A Master Class with Warren Buffett and Charlie Munger

The Q&A Sessions of the Berkshire Hathaway Inc.
Shareholders Meeting

2015

by

Eben Otuteye, PhD
and
Mohammad Siddiquee, MBA

Cover Design:

ISBN 13: 978-1512136784
ISBN 10: 1512136786

Disclaimer: This book is for educational purposes only. These notes are not verified or approved by Warren Buffett, Charlie Munger, nor by any director or officer of Berkshire Hathaway Inc. We relied primarily on our handwritten notes from the meeting. This publication is not meant to offer investment advice. No part of the information in this book should be considered a recommendation to purchase or sell any security.

Borsheim's Fine Jewelry, Omaha Photo: Mohammad Siddiquee

Table of Contents

Preface

There is no question that Warren Buffett and Charlie Munger are investment legends of our time. Over the years they have demonstrated that they are not only great investment and business managers but that they are also sages with tremendous amount of worldly wisdom that will help people to navigate life successfully.

There are countless books written about Warren Buffett and Charlie Munger's investment style and investment success. However, there are very few sources to get their thoughts and words as directly expressed by them. Usually, you get those from interviews, newspaper or magazine articles, or more directly from the annual letter to shareholders. One rich, but generally overlooked and not well-documented source of Buffett-Munger wisdom is the question and answer sessions of the annual general meeting.

It is undisputable that the AGM of Berkshire Hathaway shareholders is the one forum where they download the maximum amount of Buffett-Munger wisdom. Thus if anyone is looking for a shortcut to Buffett-Munger insight into investment, business, and life, the best advice is to go the Berkshire Shareholders Meeting or to get the transcript of the question and answer sessions—and is that what you get from this book.

Together, Warren Buffett and Charlie Munger have accumulated over 120 years of experience in investment, not counting the fact that Warren Buffett bought his first stock when he was eleven years old (six shares of Cities Services, now known as CITGO, an oil company). What makes them legends is not just the number of years of experience in active investment but also the wisdom of their modus operandi as testified to by the consistent and outstanding results delivered for over sixty years. If common sense and logic ruled the world, everyone would be investing like Warren Buffett and Charlie Munger.

We would be remiss to talk about Warren Buffett's investment acumen and prowess without acknowledging Benjamin Graham, the "Dean of Wall Street," and father of value investing. Warren always acknowledges Ben Graham as the one who had the most influence on him as an investor (for example, see Warren Buffett's answer to Question 65). Warren Buffett was Benjamin Graham's student, then became Ben Graham's employee and a lifetime family friend. Warren carefully studied and followed the principles and philosophies of Graham for years. And it only got better when he met Charlie Munger and the two of them modified and perfected that mode of investing to form their own philosophical and operational system of investment and business portfolio management.

The Master Class Series

Being relatively new to Berkshire Hathaway shareholders meeting, we thought we could prepare ourselves by reading some material on it. Apart from Warren Buffett's letters to shareholders and the Berkshire annual reports, the main resource we consulted was the book, *Pilgrimage to Warren Buffett's Omaha* by Jeff Mathews, which gave quite a good orientation. In the process we realized that there's no reliable and readily available source to access the actual Q&A sessions of past shareholders meetings. It is our opinion that majority of those who attend the meeting are keen and teachable learners who will appreciate a reference source to review the questions and answers of the meeting. Hence, the motivation for this book. We hope both Warren Buffett and Charlie Munger will stick around for a while and maintain this format of the annual meeting in order to give us the opportunity to continue to tap into their insight and wisdom.

Another motivation for the book is that both of us came to know about Warren Buffett and Charlie Munger rather late (Eben in early 2000s and Mohammad in 2010). The reason is that although we spent a lot of time in business schools, none of our instructors introduced us to his ideas (or those of Ben Graham). That is one regret we share—the lost opportunity of not knowing Warren Buffett and Charlie Munger earlier in life. We figured the way to make up for this, now that we are instructors, is to introduce our students very early in their business education to the ideas of these legendary investors. Writing this series is our way of contributing to the efforts of those who are committed to spreading the word about the right way to invest, to think about money, and to manage a business, as exemplified by Warren Buffett and Charlie Munger. We hope to use this *Master Class* series as the means to disseminate the ideas of Warren Buffett and Charlie Munger as directly enunciated and articulated by them. We believe it will be a great service not only to the investment community but to society in general.

About the Title of the Book

On May 6, 2014, Bill Gates posted a blog[1] that began:

"In the arts, a master class is a group lesson with an acknowledged expert—a chance for students to hear from an undisputed master and to improve their work by being exposed to the best.

This last weekend, I joined almost forty thousand other 'students' to attend the master class for investors that is the Berkshire Hathaway annual meeting."

That blog resonated immediately with us and we decided to use the title of the blog as the title of

[1]http://www.gatesnotes.com/About-Bill-Gates/Master-Class-with-Warren-Buffett-Berkshire-Hathaway-Annual-Meeting-2014

this book. The Berkshire Hathaway AGM is indeed a master class with legends.

Accuracy of Content

As those who attend the AGM are aware, part of the protocol is that no electronic recording equipment is permitted. Thus everything you read here was first handwritten. Although we tried to transcribe what was said as accurately as possible, we weren't able to make a verbatim copy. A number of expressions are paraphrases of what was actually said. However, we've made every effort to preserve the sense and meaning of what was said. We also consulted a number of other attendants to cross-check our notes. While our words are not always identical to others', we are satisfied that the content is an accurate representation of what was said. Of course, the punctuation is entirely our creation.

Berkshire Hathaway 2015 Annual Shareholders Meeting Notes

Saturday, May 2, 2015
CenturyLink Center
455 North 10th Street, Omaha NE 68102

Preliminaries

Opening Multimedia Show

The meeting started with a video in which Warren Buffett welcomed the shareholders to the meeting. This is a multimedia extravaganza that precedes the actual meeting.

Berkshire Hathaway shareholders meeting is popularly known as the "Woodstock of Capitalists." So we know it is not all business. In fact, it is a weekend party of believers in the ideas, values and investment practices of Warren Buffett and Charlie Munger.

The tradition is to kick things off with some entertaining movie prior to the question and answer session.

The 2015 shareholders meeting was a major milestone in the history of Berkshire Hathaway. It's been 50 years since Warren Buffett took over the leadership of the then-textile company, which has since evolved into the conglomerate that it is today[2]. The organizers went all-out this year to produce a great show to match the significance of this important milestone.

The preliminary movie is a combination of recap of segments of the history of Berkshire, together with a series of interviews, snippets to showcase either entire Berkshire Hathaway companies (subsidiaries) or individual products, in addition to skits, parodies, cartoons, and real acting by the actual people whose stories are being told to reflect the history and values of the leadership, and in some cases poke fun at personal quirks of leaders of the company.

Among many of the highlights this year was a "boxing match" that pits Warren Buffett (dubbed the "Berkshire Bomber") against Floyd Mayweather, the undefeated five-division world champion. In a well-engineered artistic fashion, we don't get to see the end of the fight as the screen suddenly gets fuzzy and scrambled before the fight ends, with Warren Buffett asking someone if they forgot to pay the cable bill.

The preliminary show also has a serious side to it. One of the well-known values of the leadership of Berkshire is that reputation is everything

---

[2] Some of the details of the evolution from a failing textile company to a very successful conglomerate are given in the Chairman's letter of the 2014 Annual Report (p. 24-38).

(addressed several times in the questions later on). In that spirit, the preliminaries usually end with Warren Buffett's opening statement before the Subcommittee on Telecommunications and Finance of the Committee on Energy and Commerce of the U.S. House of Representatives in September 1991: "Lose money for the firm and I will be understanding; lose a shred of reputation for the firm and I will be ruthless."

Q&A Format

The format of the Q&A session was similar to the last six annual meetings. Three business journalists—Andrew Ross Sorkin (CNBC and *New York Times*), Becky Quick (CNBC), and Carol Loomis (formerly with *Fortune Magazine*)—chose one-third of the questions. The rest came from shareholders and analysts. Shareholders had e-mailed over two thousand questions to the journalists, who then selected a set of questions most relevant to Berkshire and its operations.

The journalists, who were seated on the stage, alternated with analysts Gary Ransom (Dowling & Partners), Gregg Warren (Morningstar), and Jonathan Brandt (Ruane, Cunniff & Goldfarb) and with shareholders in the audience in asking the questions.

<u>Notations</u>

Warren: Warren Buffett, Chairman and CEO of Berkshire Hathaway Inc.
Charlie: Charlie Munger, Vice Chairman of Berkshire Hathaway Inc.
Matt: Matt Rose, Executive Chairman of BNSF
Greg: Greg Abel, CEO of Berkshire Hathaway Energy
BNSF: Burlington Northern Santa Fe

Preliminary Remarks from Warren Buffett

Warren: Good morning. Hi, I'm Warren. This is Charlie. He can hear, I can see. We work together.

Before we start, two very special guests have to stand up. Hollywood director John Landis for the part of the movie with Floyd Mayweather [applause from audience] and Carrie Sova, who organized everything here today; please thank Carrie Sova [applause]. She has a one and a half-year-old boy. I asked Carrie whether she could come up with a commemorative book for our 50th year anniversary. She printed 15,000 copies of the book and 100 percent of the credit goes to her. I would like to thank her [applause].

We will be done with the question and answer session by 3:30 p.m. We'll have the shareholders' meeting after the Q&A. We'll recess for fifteen minutes, then at 3:45 p.m. begin the shareholders' meeting. For those who are still looking for seats, there may be some seats in the overflow rooms we created at the Hilton [which is across from the CenturyLink Center]. We got all the places that we could.

Now I'll introduce the Board of Directors in alphabetical order, but please hold your applause until I'm finished introducing them. After the introductions, if you like, you can still hold your applause. In alphabetical order: Howard Buffett [President of Buffett Farms], Steve Burke [CEO of NBCUniversal], Susan Decker [former President of Yahoo! Inc.], Bill Gates [Co-Chair of the Bill and Melinda Gates Foundation], David Gottesman [Senior Managing Director of First Manhattan Company], Charlotte Guyman [former Chairman of the Board of Directors of UM Medicine], Charlie Munger [Vice Chairman of Berkshire], Tom Murphy [former Chairman of the Board and CEO of Capital Cities/ABC], Ron Olson [Partner of the law firm of Munger, Tolles & Olson LLP], Walter Scott [Chairman of Level 3 Communications], Meryl Witmer [Managing member of the General Partner of Eagle Capital Partners L.P.]. That is the Board of Directors of Berkshire [applause].

We are missing Don Keough. He died a couple of weeks ago. He used to sell coffee and broadcast Nebraska football games. There was another guy with him doing a fifteen-minute radio show after his show.[3] He always asked me what happened to this Carson fellow.

---

[3] Don Keough hosted a TV talk show called "Coffee Counter" just

We have his wife, Mickie Keough, with us today. Mickie, would you please stand up? [applause]. Don was very busy and Mickie did most of the heavy lifting of bringing up their kids. So if you find any faults in them you can blame Mickie.

We have a couple of slides, then we'll move into questions until noon, back at 1 p.m., continue until 3:30 p.m. We released our earnings yesterday [Friday, May 1, 2015]. We try to do that on a Friday so you have a full weekend to digest the 10-Q which we make available [Form 10-Q is used for quarterly reports under Section 13 or 15(d) of the Securities Exchange Act of 1934]. This is our summary slide for Q1; nothing particularly remarkable [1st quarter slide shown on projector]. The railroad did dramatically better. We're going to spend a lot of money, making sure that things get better [at the railroad]. I want to thank Matt Rose and Carl Ice[4] for that. I am happy to see the result.

[Someone from the audience said, "Warren and Charlie, we love you." Mr. Buffett says: "I didn't quite get it, but I'll assume it was complimentary."]

---

before "Carson's Corner," but moved into the advertising side of the business, landing a job with Paxton & Gallagher, maker of Butter-Nut Coffee. Through a series of purchases, the company became part of Coca-Cola's food division. http://www.omaha.com/money/creighton-grad-donald-keough-ex-coca-cola-president-with-deep/article_7ae3c378-bc63-11e4-890a-8342c8dd447e.html

[4] President and CEO of BNSF Railway. Ice has been at the railroad for thirty-four years, and has been president of BNSF since November 2010. He became CEO on January 1, 2014.

We'll handle questions from the journalists, then analysts, and finally from the audience, and alternate. We'll break for lunch at 12 and come back at 1. There are sixty-six questions in total. The questions are selected by a drawing. Neither Charlie nor I knew any of these questions.

"If fifty people can get a job done, no one is better off if a hundred people do the job."
Warren Buffett

"If people weren't often so wrong, we wouldn't be so rich."
Charlie Munger

"We think any company that employs an economist has one employee too many."
Warren Buffett

Questions and Answers: Part 1

Q1. Carol Loomis: We received hundreds of questions in the last two months. Both Warren and Charlie had no idea what questions would be asked. Sorry if we missed your question. The first question is from a shareholder from Texas:

"I have been a shareholder for fifteen years but now I am suffering from heartburn. I thought Berkshire Hathaway was an ethical company. But two things call that into question:

(1) the *Seattle Times* [newspaper] article on the predatory lending practices of Clayton Homes, a manufactured-housing unit that Berkshire owns, and (2) growing partnership with 3G Capital, a private-equity firm that Berkshire has partnered with in a few deals.

I cannot make the moral case for you and 3G coming together and I don't know how you can do so. I am deeply disappointed in Berkshire's association with them. Both of you have avoided anti-social business practices in the past. I wonder how you can defend your association with these firms?"

Warren: I'm clearly prepared for the Clayton question. I make no apologies whatsoever for Clayton's lending practices. Clayton is not unethical. Clayton has behaved very well. I read the article in the *Seattle Times*.[5] There is an important mistake.

The mortgage lending at Clayton is exemplary and extraordinary. Unlike most mortgage lenders, Clayton keeps its mortgages. Clayton doesn't sell them to third parties.

The problem in the housing bubble of early 2006 to 2008 was that the mortgage holder got divorced from the mortgage originator and the home builder. The originator packaged and securitized the loans so people around the world had no connection to the original transaction. You had these two parties with no connection to the actual outcome of whether it was a good mortgage or not.

When a mortgage goes bad, three parties lose: the home buyer, the mortgage company, and the [securitized] mortgage investor. Clayton does not resell its mortgages. Clayton keeps 100 percent of the mortgage and therefore has the same risk as the home buyer. If a mortgage goes bad, both Clayton and the homeowner lose. So with default, Clayton has the same interest that society and the homeowner have, not to make loans to people that are going to get into trouble. At Clayton, we retained roughly $12 billion of mortgages on 300,000 homes.

There's been much talk in terms of changes in mortgage rules to get the originators to keep some

---

[5] "The mobile-home trap: How a Warren Buffett empire preys on the poor." http://www.seattletimes.com/business/real-estate/the-mobile-home-trap-how-a-warren-buffett-empire-preys-on-the-poor/

skin in the game...just so they would have an interest in these mortgages.

Of homes selling for less than $150,000, 70 percent of them are manufactured. The mortgage applicants for these usually have low FICO scores.[6] Reality is that many borrowers for manufactured housing don't qualify with a traditional FICO score, so they're riskier borrowers.

About 3 percent of the mortgages default. When they do, we lose money and the person that bought the house loses money. But 97 percent don't and most of those people wouldn't be living in these kinds of housing without the financing that Clayton and others make available.

The rate of failed mortgages made through Clayton is minimal. Without the lending efforts made through the organization, these people wouldn't be enjoying home ownership in the first place.

If we make a mistake, it hurts them and it hurts us.

I would like to invite you to visit the $69,500, 1,200 square feet Clayton-manufactured home at the exhibition hall. For $69,500 you get a nice home with everything, appliances and all. You need another

---

[6] Founded in 1956, Fair Isaac Corporation (NYSE: FICO) is a credit rating analytics software company. The company operates in three segments, such as Applications, Scores, and Tools.

$25,000 for land and other expenses. With $95,000 you are getting a decent home. We help people to move to their own homes. If we make any mistake that hurts them, it hurts us as well.

I read the story in the *Seattle Times*. There's a part of the story that is not true. I disagree with the part about Clayton that attributes comments from an executive in a 2012 affidavit about Clayton's profit margin. I searched the affidavit and I think the story mistook gross margins for net profit margins—which are much smaller. I think anyone who understands accounting wouldn't make that mistake.

Here is a slide on the difference between gross profit margin and after-tax profit margin [Warren Buffett shows a table of numbers on the projector]. As you can see in this slide, the numbers from Macy's and Target and also the number from Clayton Homes [gross profit margin 20 percent, pre-tax margin 3 percent and after-tax margin 2 percent]. Gross profit margins are very different from net profit margins.

Clayton has a simplified lending system. In the next slide, you can see a simple one-page lender form. There are no fine prints. Homeowners can borrow money from local banks and we also lend money. I have never received any calls or complaints from anyone about Clayton Homes.

Every year, we write about 300,000 loans. We are regulated in almost every state in which we have financing. Every state has its own examination policies. Clayton operates in a market that is regulated in nineteen states. In the last three years, we have had I think ninety-one examinations by the states. They look at our practices and make sure they conform to the laws. So far, the largest fine we ever received was $5,500. We also had to refund $110,000. When we can't lend, we direct people to FHA loans.[7] Ninety-seven percent of the homeowners we lend to have FICO scores below 620, with the average principal and interest payments approximating $600 a month.

Charlie: I don't know a lot about the mortgage practices at Clayton Homes. But I always wondered why manufactured homes don't have a bigger share of the market. You can't make lending to poor people buying houses 100 percent successful.

Warren: Credit and home ownership are subject to job loss, divorce, death, etc. Those things hurt everyone but they have greater impact on the low-income end of the market.

Regarding 3G Capital, you cannot find any statement by Charlie or me where we recommend to have more people working in a company than needed. If fifty people can get a job done, no one is better off if a hundred people do the job. 3G has had

---

[7] Federal Housing Administration, a federal government agency created as part of the National Housing Act of 1934 to improve housing standards and conditions, provide an adequate home financing system through insurance of mortgage loans, and to stabilize the mortgage market. http://www.fha.gov

some of those cases and once they reduce the number of head counts the company does very well; for example, Heinz and Tim Hortons. Both Burger King and Tim Hortons did well in the first quarter under 3G's management. Good companies will not employ more people than they need. The businesses under 3G are well managed and that makes sense to us.

Charlie: The system of having a company with the right number of people works very well. In Russia under the Communists, everyone had a job. Then some workers say, "They pretend to pay us and we pretend to work." Of course, we want the right number of people in the right number of jobs.

Warren: That's exactly what happened in the railroad business in the 1940s. It was a lousy business with 1.6 million people working. Now with less than 200,000 people, they have better cars, we do more business, and we cover longer distances with higher safety.

Efficiency is required over time in capitalism. I really tip my hat to the 3G people for what they have done.

Q2. Jonathan Brandt from Ruane, Cunniff & Goldfarb: The question is about Van Tuyl, the car-dealership chain Berkshire recently bought. When its competitors like CarMax and AutoNation emphasize fixed and low prices, will Van Tuyl go for a new sales model where the consumers will know what price they'll pay for a

car before they get to the lot? Do you think the traditional way of selling cars will continue or will things change?

Warren: I don't know what system will prevail. If change is required, it will be done. Auto dealership will evolve to what the customer wants. I don't know what will happen to auto dealership in the future but I will not be surprised if there is no change in the next five to ten years. Negotiations are going on in a lot of businesses. Van Tuyl will adopt whatever is required—whatever customers want. But I won't be surprised if it remains the same.

I can't predict how much Van Tuyl will make next year but I am sure it will be quite profitable.

Charlie: The car-dealership business model has been amazingly resistant to change in my lifetime. I think we can do a lot more like it [Van Tuyl].

Warren: [to Charlie] You think you will be negotiating on car dealerships ten years from now?

Charlie: When people are dealing with big-ticket items they like to negotiate.

Warren: Real estate has at times been under the same pressure, but that business model has endured too. It happens when you buy jewelry, when you buy a home. When people are dealing with big-ticket items, a lot of people's natural tendency is to negotiate, and they'll do so if they think it's built into the system.

Q3. Station 1, Shareholder: Can you name five characteristics that give you confidence in predicting the earnings of a company ten years from now?

Warren: Charlie, what are your five picks?

Charlie: We don't have a one-size-fits-all system to buy firms. Businesses are different. Every industry is different and we also keep learning. What we did ten years ago, we hope we are doing better now. We can't give you a formula.

Warren: I don't have a list of five characteristics, but I like companies where I have a reasonable idea of how they might look in five years.

What we think about is what stops us from going ahead. We consider a few important questions, such as whether the owner of the business is available to manage the business, and do we really want to be in partnership with this person and count on them to behave well in the future. That stops a fair number of deals.

We don't have a list of five. If we do, Charlie has kept it from me.

Q4. Becky Quick from CNBC: You talked about "cigar butt"[8] approach before. Do you think IBM

---

[8] "Cigar butt" was a term coined by Warren Buffett to describe

is a cigar butt case? Did Charlie talk you out of buying IBM?

Charlie: The answer is No. Berkshire has owned lots of companies with temporary reversals and IBM is a very unique company. It's very rare that when technology changes both people and the company adapt. IBM totally dominated the punch cards business and then adapted as computing changed to a new system. It's very rare in tech companies. IBM is a very credible company. It's still an enormous enterprise and admirable company. It helps that Berkshire bought the stock at a reasonable price.

Warren: When we bought IBM, it was a 2–0 vote.

I never understand why people expect us to talk up Berkshire investments. It's the mentality of Wall Street.

If we talked our book, we would say pessimistic things about all four of the biggest holdings we have, because all four are repurchasing their shares at the moment.

We have no interest in encouraging people to buy what we buy. If people buy what we buy, the price goes up and that is not in our interest. People don't seem to get that.

companies bought at significant discount: "A cigar butt found on the street that has only one puff left in it may not offer much of a smoke, but the 'bargain purchase' (free) will make that puff all profit" (Warren Buffett's 1989 letter to Berkshire shareholders).

Charlie: If people weren't often so wrong, we wouldn't be so rich.

Q5. Gary Ransom from Dowling & Partners: In Charlie Munger's 50[9]th year anniversary letter, he mentioned that Buffett got lucky in several instances over the past five decades since taking the helm at Berkshire. Do you agree that you cannot repeat that success today?

Warren: I have many instances of luck but especially with insurance. I got lucky three times in the insurance business:

1. On a Saturday, when I was twenty years old, I received some four hours of education in insurance business from a GEICO executive. Lorimer Davidson[10] gave me education that I couldn't have got from any American business school.
2. In 1967, I got lucky again when we bought National Indemnity. Jack Ringwalt[11] got mad

[9] You can read the letter, Vice Chairman's Thoughts – Past and Future here (page 39):
http://www.berkshirehathaway.com/letters/2014ltr.pdf

[10] Lorimer Davidson, an investment banker, joined GEICO in 1948 and expanded its pool of investors; replaced Leo Goodwin, the founder of GEICO in 1958.

[11] "Jack Ringwalt, a friend of mine who was the controlling shareholder of the two companies, came to my office saying he would like to sell. Fifteen minutes later, we had a deal. Neither of Jack's companies had ever had an audit by a public accounting firm, and I didn't ask for one. My reasoning: (1) Jack was honest

about something and wanted to sell his business. I couldn't have done it an hour later as Ringwalt would have likely changed his mind as he had done in the past.

3. In the mid-1980s on a Saturday, when I met Ajit Jain saying he never had any experience in insurance business. How luckier can you get?

The odds are very much against being able to pull off a trifecta like that in the future. You couldn't expect to have three lucky events like that happen again.

The whole thing in business is being open to ideas as they come along. Insurance is something I could understand and appreciate. Lots of accidents happen. If you keep yourself open then good accidents will happen.

But if I were starting over again, I would rather find something other than insurance to direct my attention to.

Charlie: I don't think we would have that kind of success anymore. Berkshire created its reinsurance business in Omaha, and it has turned into a huge a business.

---

and (2) he was also a bit quirky and likely to walk away if the deal became at all complicated" (Warren Buffett's 2014 letter to Berkshire shareholders, available here: http://www.berkshirehathaway.com/letters/2014ltr.pdf).

Q6. Station 2, Shareholder from Germany: In my home country you are regarded as a role model of integrity. Berkshire has a unique culture. How can we judge Berkshire once you two depart?

Warren: I think you should be pleased with Berkshire's culture after we are gone. Berkshire's culture runs as deep as any large company.

It is interesting that you are from Germany because three or four days ago, we closed a deal with a German lady, Mrs. Louis[12] for 400 million euros ($452 million).

Mrs. Louis wanted to sell her business to Berkshire because of its culture. Now, thirty or forty years ago, she might not want to sell her business to us. We have deeply embedded values and a deeply embedded culture. I expect it will continue and become even stronger.

If you have 97 percent of shareholders voting not to have dividends that says something. We try to define and make clear the culture of the business. We behave consistently. Some people like it and some shun us. We have directors who want to contribute. We have directors who see their role as a great opportunity for stewardship, rather than serving as directors for the money.

---

[12] Mrs. Ute Louis, the owner of Detlev Louis Motorradvertriebs GmbH, a motorcycle apparel and accessories retailer in Germany. https://www.louis.eu

Charlie: Once we're gone, it'll become clear that it's not the force of personality that's driving Berkshire. It's institutionalized. And it will continue for decades and decades and decades to come. I said in the annual report that Berkshire will do well, maybe even better in dollar terms.

We will never gain as much in percentage terms as we did in the beginning years. There are worse tragedies in life than having Berkshire's growth slow down a little.

Warren: Name one!

Charlie: What happened in Salomon, I don't like anybody doing that. We couldn't have turned Salomon into Berkshire. It doesn't mean Berkshire is a monastery.

Warren: Berkshire has many capable managers. They are more concerned about what is good for Berkshire than what they can get for themselves.

Q7. Andrew Ross Sorkin from the *New York Times*: With the increasingly known adverse health effects of high sugar consumption and changing consumer habits, the shareholder asks if we've reached an inflection point in the American consumer and, specifically, if Coca-Cola and Heinz's moats are narrowing?

Warren: You will not see any revolutionary change in the food and beverage sector. But I think all food and beverage companies will adjust to the expressed preferences of the consumers. No company ever does well ignoring its customer.

Coca-Cola has a wide economic moat stemming from the company's iconic brand image, strong distribution network, and economies of scale. Twenty years from now, I predict there will be more Coke cases consumed than now by some margin. In the 1940s, folks said Coke's growth was over. In 1988, when we bought Coke shares, people again were not enthused over the company's profitability. One-quarter of all the calories I have consumed came from Coca-Cola. But I'm not sure which quarter.

Although recent carbonated soft-drink declines will probably continue in developed markets and we've seen macro economic concerns, which have threatened near-term growth opportunities, we expect gains in emerging and international markets over the long run.

There's a lot to be said about being happy with what you're doing. If I lived my whole life eating broccoli and Brussels sprout, I probably wouldn't live as long.

[Then Mr. Buffett subtly picks up the box of See's Candies on the table in front of him and passes it to Mr. Munger] [Crowd laughing]. Eating broccoli is like going to jail.

Charlie: There's no question about it; sugar is enormously useful. Sugar prevents premature softening of the arteries. If it shortens my life, I've avoided a few months dribbling at a nursing home.

Warren: I have enjoyed every meal I had except at my grandfather's when he made me eat those damn green vegetables.

There are some shifts in preferences but it's remarkable how we like the brands we buy. At one point, we were the largest shareholders of General Foods 30-plus years ago.

Heinz brands go back to 1869. Ketchup came out in the 1870s. Coke brands go back to 1886. It's a pretty good bet that people will still be liking the same things [in the future].

When I compare drinking Coke to something that someone would sell me from Whole Foods, ... I don't see a lot of smiles on the faces of people at Whole Foods.

Q8. Gregg Warren: Talking about auto dealership, in the long run you need to build scale in the auto-dealership business. Do you think getting more auto dealers will give Berkshire scale?

Warren: There aren't huge economies of scale in dealerships but running dealerships well is critical. I don't think you widen profit margins by having a thousand dealers versus having fewer. Scale doesn't matter much in cars because local dealers develop local reputations, so it's all about the quality of the dealerships you own. There are seventeen thousand dealers in the country. If you ask people to name dealers, they come up with local names. You don't gain much by having a huge number of dealerships.

We go for local dealerships that are well managed, since people tend to prefer local dealers. We will be behind many dealers in the future. We hope to own the local operations that are doing very well.

The banks are the natural lenders to dealers. We don't see ourselves getting into financing like other companies, for example, Wells Fargo, which has cost advantage. Berkshire can't borrow at a low rate like the banks. So we're not going to be in the financing business. We will be looking for auto dealers—local business, not a giant operation.

Charlie: Van Tuyl has a system of meritocracy, where the right person gets the power and ownership. The right people are prospering in Van Tuyl. It reminds me a lot of the Kiewit Corp.[13] here in Omaha, where the right people are in power. They

[13] Established in 1884 by Peter Kiewit, Kiewit Corp. is one of North America's largest and most respected construction and engineering organizations. The employee-owned company operates through a network of offices and projects in the United States, Canada, and Australia.

are "kissing cousins" in terms of culture. They both have a very good thing going for them with the right people prospering.

Q9. Station 3, Shareholder, Connecticut: This is a follow-up on culture and stewardship. We're just getting started with our company. We discuss values and culture quite a bit. I cherish the culture and stewardship in Berkshire. I would like some tips from fifty years ago when you started Berkshire.

Warren: Culture has to come from the top and be consistent. It has to be communicated, talked about and practiced. It is a grain of sand type of thing. People see what you do rather than what you say. People see how those above them behave and they move in that direction. You reward for performance and punish people for their wrongdoings.

Obviously, it's much easier to do if you inherit a culture you like and it's easier in small firms. Children see what you do, not what you say. At Berkshire, with about 340,000 people, I am sure at any given time there is someone doing something he should not be doing.

I made a couple of tweaks to some practices at Clayton Homes and Kirby. In case of Clayton Homes, I told them I don't like thirty-year mortgages, so I stopped it. I didn't like some of the sales practices I saw at Kirby, so we changed them. We especially didn't like seeing how some seniors were being treated in sales processes, so we instituted a policy to protect them. Now if you are over sixty-five and you bought a Kirby vacuum cleaner, you have 100 percent money-back guarantee within a full year.

The same with GEICO—we always try to make our customers feel satisfied and content. Of the millions of claims settled by GEICO, it's not often where two people involved in an accident agree, but we try to behave as if our positions are reversed.

[Within the Berkshire companies] I arranged a golden handshake program so that some people can leave. We're far from perfect, but if you keep working at it, it does get results. I want people to write to me if they notice anything wrong going on.

Charlie: One thing we did best was that we were always dissatisfied with what we already knew. We always wanted to know more. So we kept learning. I don't think that will ever stop. If we stayed frozen in time (particularly Warren), Berkshire would have been a terrible place.

Q10. Carol Loomis: This question is about two indicators: (1) the percentage of total market cap relative to the U.S. GNP and (2) corporate profit as percentage of GNP. Market cap as percentage of GNP is now about 125 percent (about the same as 1999 just before the bubble burst). Corporate profit as percentage of GNP was between 4 percent and 6.5 percent from 1951 to 1999. Right now [as of Friday, May 1, 2015] it is about 10.5 percent, way above the normal levels.

Do you think the current levels of either one relative to overall growth should be a matter of concern to the general investing public?[14]

Warren: The second one—corporate profit as a percentage of GDP—should be of concern to investors in general. American business is prospering.

Regarding the first one, we live in a low interest rate environment, which makes historical valuation comparison challenging.

Corporate profits are worth a whole lot more with government bonds at 1 percent than at 5 percent. Stocks are selling at historically high prices, but you need to look at them in the context of interest rates—the opportunity cost of owning bonds vs. stocks.

We live in a world that has incredibly low interest rates and stocks are selling at historically high prices. The question is how long will these rates prevail? Will we be like Japan? Japan has been in a similar situation for a long period of time. If we continue with low interest rates, stocks will look very cheap.

I can't recall us making an acquisition or turning down one because of macro factors. We

---

[14] The question provided to Carol Loomis used "GNP" but Warren Buffett answered with GDP; GDP is the more appropriate metric.

bought Burlington Northern at a time of terrible general economic conditions. When we bought See's Candies, we didn't know whether that would work. But that doesn't block us from buying any companies.

What we knew was that we didn't know what the macro environment would be like. But we look at the average profitability of the company. We think any company that employs an economist has one employee too many.

Charlie, can you think of anything not rude to say that I haven't said?

Charlie: It would be hard to improve on that one.

" … every time we've used stock as a purchase tool,
it's been a mistake."
Charlie Munger

"I will not take 1 percent chance with my Aunt
Katie's [or anybody's] net worth."
Warren Buffett

Q11. Jonathan Brandt: It's about new rules for railroad tank car safety. They were unveiled after much work in Washington this week. The question is how do these rules affect Berkshire which owns a railroad company like BNSF and a railcar manufacturer like Marmon? How do you think the new rule will strike a balance between safety and efficiency?

Warren: You've asked all the questions I'll be asking. The document came out two days ago and it consists of more than three hundred pages.[15] I haven't read them yet. So I don't know enough about them to answer.

I've talked with Matt Rose and Frank Ptak[16] briefly about them. The interests of their businesses—BNSF and our tank car manufacturer, Marmon—may diverge at times. We bought the safest tank cars. As a common carrier, we are required to carry ammonia and chlorine and other dangerous materials that we would rather not be carrying using railroad.

---

[15] Developed by the Pipeline and Hazardous Materials Safety Administration (PHMSA) and Federal Railroad Administration (FRA), in coordination with Canada, the new rule focuses on safety improvements designed to prevent accidents, mitigate consequences in the event of an accident, and support emergency response.
http://www.transportation.gov/sites/dot.gov/files/docs/final-rule-flammable-liquids-by-rail_0.pdf

[16] Mr. Frank S. Ptak, CFA has been the Chief Executive Officer and President of The Marmon Group LLC, a Berkshire subsidiary since January 3, 2006.

Clearly we and the country have an interest in developing safer cars. Some cars we thought were safe were less so than we thought. I believe people will be somewhat unhappy with the rules. But it is up to Washington to make rules that will improve safety.

You are going to have derailments but you better have cars that will be safe in the face of a derailment. BNSF is leading the industry when it comes to safety. But nothing will be perfect.

Charlie: Big companies like BNSF, ExxonMobil, and Chevron have a lot of engineers working on safety. None of that's going to change. You'd be out of your mind to think these big companies do not pay close attention to safety.

Warren: The Bakken crude has shown to be more volatile than other crude.

Charlie: It's almost a misnomer to call it crude.

Warren: BNSF has the best safety record in the industry. BH Energy has a remarkable safety record. At every subsidiary we've acquired, Greg Abel has ensured that their safety has gotten better.

Charlie: Before we bought Omaha pipeline, it was mismanaged. We worked days and nights to improve it. Nobody wanted to see another pipeline explosion. We went from last to the first or second position.

Q12. Shareholder, Station 4: What advice would you give to someone who doesn't have access to the alumni network of a top business school?

Charlie: I'll take that one. I think you should do the best you can. Play the hand you've got.

Warren: Charlie is very much Old Testament. He didn't get much past Genesis.

Charlie: I never had any business school training. Why should you have any?

Warren: I'd say that business school training was even a handicap twenty years ago. They teach efficient market hypothesis in the business school. Imagine paying $30,000 to $40,000 a year to hear that.

Charlie: You are very lucky avoiding what you've avoided.

Warren: How about law school, Charlie?

Charlie: I asked one of my grandchildren attending law school and he said it's like a pie eating contest. If you win, you get more pie to eat.

Q13. Becky Quick of CNBC: One potential risk to BNSF is a large railroad accident. Recently there have been some accidents in rural areas, but how would it affect the company if it

happened in an urban area? Is BNSF insured against such accidents?

Warren: Our reinsurance business went to four major railroads and offered very high limits without success. If you had the perfect circumstances for a terrible disaster, it could be calamitous.

When you run rails millions and millions of miles every year, something is bound to happen. You try to minimize risks, and work to be safer. Very small probability, but you will never be perfectly safe.

We run trains slower in urban areas as has been instituted when transporting crude oil. But we will never be perfectly safe, although we have some of the highest safety rankings at BNSF.

I don't anticipate buying five thousand new railcars. Marmon has taken on a new facility that we expect will be working three shifts at retrofitting cars (our own and those of others) to meet the new federal requirements. The industry had to wait to find out what the rules would be.

We have some insurance at BNSF, but we don't need insurance at Berkshire; we have the capacity to take on any risk that comes along. We aren't net consumers of insurance; we're selling it. We offered it at very high rates to the major railroads, but nobody wanted to pay.

In the first quarter of 2015, there were no tank car orders. We will be very active in the tank car business in the future. But historically, railroad companies have not owned tank cars.

Q14. Gary Ransom, Dowling & Partners: This question is about intra-company transactions among insurance companies. There are lots of activities in some of the Berkshire subsidiaries transferring cash to GEICO or to National Indemnity. It seems like a lot more activity than normal, so what's the purpose of these movements and why now?

Warren: A lot of things at Berkshire can be answered by "because we just got around to it." It makes it simpler to have fewer pockets to look at for capital. It really makes life easier in terms of managing money if most of the funds are concentrated in National Indemnity. It's an extra layer of capital. But all the money will be invested.

There is no real change in policies. Berkshire wants to keep every place loaded with more capital than anyone could possibly conceive of us needing and that's probably going to result in more of the funds being concentrated in National Indemnity. GEICO is also loaded with capital.

Q15. Shareholder, Station 5: The question is about the Asian Infrastructure Investment Bank and why the U.S. multinationals haven't joined?

Warren: That's a subject I know absolutely nothing about. Charlie?

Charlie: I know less than you do.

Warren: If we started talking about it, we'd be bluffing. Do you have any other question?

Shareholder: How about the future of the dollar as a reserve currency?

Warren: I have a feeling on that subject. I think the dollar will be the world's reserve currency years from now.

Charlie: I'm more nervous when lots of people print and spend money. I like it better when we print money to build infrastructure than when we print money to spread around with a helicopter.

Warren: Helicopter?

Charlie: Silence [as he turns to Warren].

Q16. Andrew Ross Sorkin: Berkshire has renamed a couple of businesses so they have the Berkshire name. For example, Van Tuyl, which is now called Berkshire Hathaway Automotive, and real estate brokerage operation, which they purchased from Prudential, is Berkshire Hathaway HomeServices. Discuss the risks associated with using the Berkshire name. Is it an attempt to add value to those businesses? Will the practice continue in other units as well? Will Fruit of the Loom become Berkshire Undergarments?

Warren: Berkshire HomeServices is a franchise operation. We bought two-thirds of the Prudential franchise and we will be buying the remaining one-third in a couple of years. We use the Berkshire name in part because Berkshire is going to lose the right to use the Prudential name at that time.

Subsidiaries may like to use the Berkshire brand, but I asked them not to abuse it. We don't want Berkshire to be a household name.

Individual outlets of Van Tuyl's car dealerships can use the Berkshire name, but Berkshire can yank their rights to use it if they abuse it. It's a bit of a carrot-and-stick thing to encourage good behavior. If they use the Berkshire name and something goes wrong, I will get on them faster than if they were not using the name.

I am aware that some subsidiaries use "A Berkshire Hathaway company" on their letterhead and it's just fine.

Charlie: It would be crazy to start selling Berkshire peanut brittle instead of See's.

Warren: There will always be fights between retailers and brands. The brand has to stand for something in the consumer's mind.

Private labels have been around forever. I recall when Sam Walton sent me the first six-pack of Sam's Cola. A brand needs to be nourished. RC Cola came up with the first diet product in the 60s. Despite private brands, Gillette ends up with 70 percent of the dollar value of razors thanks to their strong brand. It is important to protect the brand in all ways. The great brands will survive.

Q17. Gregg Warren from Morningstar: This question is about renewable energy. Elon Musk of Tesla Motors is coming up with battery for the home. How long do you believe it will be before distributed generation becomes a threat to utilities?

Warren: Charlie knows it better than I do. Renewable energy is something Berkshire pays a lot of attention to. The best defense is to have low-cost energy. People who have adopted solar in our territories have been minuscule. But huge improvements in storage would make a difference in a lot of ways.

Charlie: Obviously, we're going to use a lot more renewable energy because fossil fuels aren't going to last forever. I grew up in this part of the world, and we have 20 percent of BH Energy utilities energy coming from wind. Berkshire is very aggressive and well located.

It's not a threat, it's a huge benefit to humanity, and I think it'll be a huge benefit to

Berkshire. What the hell would we do, if we run out of fossil fuel? There will be more opportunity in the storage business than disruption.

Warren: Just in the last week we've announced our first wind farm in Nebraska, and we're adding a whole lot more in Iowa. It's a moving target. Greg [Abel] will give you some updates on renewable energy projects Berkshire undertook in Iowa.

Greg: Berkshire announced its tenth project (4,000 megawatts) in Iowa. We will have 58 percent of the company's energy coming from wind by the end of 2016. The company has more than $18 billion committed to retirement of coal facilities in Indiana. We are committed to retire 76 percent of coal at NV Energy to replace it with renewable sources. There are great opportunities for all of our utilities, and we'll embrace them.

Charlie: Do you think we have more disruption to fear or more opportunity to love?

Greg: We have a lot of opportunity ahead.

Warren: Wind and solar development are dependent on tax credits for now. The market system wouldn't produce the amount society wants without the tax credits, but because BH Energy is part of the parent company, the tax credits allow us to make much more use of those credits than would have made sense if it were nonconsolidated with the parent company. That makes it by far the biggest player in renewable energy, and circumstances are set to compound that, since other utilities have less incentive to invest in wind and solar because they don't have the same kind of taxable income.

Q18. Shareholder, Station 6: Looking back on the last fifty years, what was your most memorable failure, and how did you deal with it?

Warren: In the mid-90s I paid $400 million for Dexter Shoes[17] that was destined to go to zero in a few years. And I paid in stock that would now be worth $6 billion. It makes me feel better when our stock price goes down because it makes me feel less stupid. Nobody misled us. I just made a mistake in my assessment.

Charlie: Of course, every time we've used stock as a purchase tool, it's been a mistake.

Warren: We've had our own net worth and our families' net worth and our friends and partners put net worth into the partnership. We've been very, very cautious about what we've done. So there have been times we could have stretched a little harder and

---

[17] Harold Alfond (March 6, 1914 – November 16, 2007) founded Dexter Shoes in 1957 in Dexter, Maine to manufacture shoes for private label catalog market. Dexter has been renowned for its tradition of quality, versatility, and value; sells bowling shoes these days. In 1993, Alfond sold Dexter and its affiliates, Pan Am Shoe and Ocsap Ltd. for $433 million in stock to Berkshire Hathaway. Warren admitted in 2008 that it was the worst deal that he has ever made. http://www.dexterbowling.com

pushed a bit more. I will not take 1 percent chance with my Aunt Katie's net worth.

People will say if we do this, we will miss some opportunities, and it's just fine.

Charlie: We would get a lot bigger if we had used the leverage that other successful businesses used. But we would have sweat at night. And it's crazy to sweat at night.

Warren: Over financial matters?

Charlie: Yes, over financial matters.

Q19. Carol Loomis: You warned in the 2008 letter of the possibility of high inflation and the consequence for Berkshire relative to other large companies. Do you think that is still possible?

Warren: So far, I've been very wrong. Charlie's been a little bit wrong. I would not have predicted that you could have five or six years of rates close to zero (and even negative right now in Europe), and sustain deficits, and not raise the ratio of debt to GDP.

Charlie: Of course.

Warren: Deficits aren't a dirty word, but large ones are scary. The Federal Reserve's balance sheet is well outside what we discussed in my Economics 101 course, and the only real negative consequence is that savers have just been killed. If the money supply grows and grows, I don't know how you don't have inflation.

I think we operate in a world where Charlie and I don't understand very well. Poland issuing bonds with negative interest rates is just something I never would have anticipated.

Berkshire will be positioned well to be strong even in strange times. We will remain poised to act on our own at any time. We're sitting on $60 billion of cash right now; I'd rather have $20 billion and one great $40 billion acquisition. If any kind of economic turbulence occurs, I want to be ready for it when a lot of people won't be.

Charlie: We made little progress by trying to outguess the macro predictions.

Warren: We don't see any benefit to those who make all these macro predictions. They get a lot of airtime, but they don't make a lot of money. That's all.

Charlie: We just keep swimming and let the tide take care of itself. The problem with making economic forecasts is that people make them long enough, and they start to believe they know something. It's much better to just say you are ignorant.

Warren: We will occasionally see things that make sense for Berkshire, and we'll remain prepared both financially and psychologically.

Q20. Jonathan Brandt: Berkshire has a big gap between cash and reported taxes. How do you view this gap? Is it economic earnings?

Warren: There are two forms of float from taxes. One is the unrealized appreciation of assets. The other is accelerated depreciation, which has been around forever. Berkshire's $37 billion in deferred taxes should be viewed as permanent float. The unrealized appreciation of securities is part of the deferred taxes. These gains could be realized over time.

Accelerated depreciation has been around a long time in the utility business, which helps our customer but it doesn't really help us. We get a return on equity, but it's not "free" equity, and the regulators take it into account. There's less cash going out the door, and that reduces our need for cash for capital investment, but it's not a hidden form of equity.

Charlie: If corporate tax rates change, it would be a book entry and not mean so much.

Warren: We regard the float from the insurance business as a huge asset but deferred taxes not so much.

"The idea of running a fat operation just because you're profitable is crazy."
Warren Buffett

"If you can behave like a young investor, evaluate stocks like businesses, and invest when things are very cheap (no matter what the people on TV say), you will do very well."
Warren Buffett

"Value investing will never go out of style. Who the hell doesn't want value when they're buying things? Why do we want it everywhere but in stocks?"
Charlie Munger

"Trustworthiness is more important than the brain. We wouldn't hire anybody, no matter how able they were, if we didn't trust them."
Charlie Munger

Q21. Shareholder, Station 5: Can you speak to your knowledge of Teledyne?

Warren: Charlie knew and studied Henry Singleton[18] personally. There's a lot to be learned from Singleton in his operating years, and from what happened after.

Charlie: Henry Singleton was a lot smarter than Warren or me. He aced his tests and could play chess blindfolded. Singleton looked only at initial guidance, but Warren worked harder and got better results. Singleton had very clever incentives that he applied to his executives. The incentives got so strong and the culture of performance got so strong that the people inside Teledyne went too far in dealing with the Defense Department and got the company in trouble.

Warren: We believe a lot in the power of incentives. But we've seen more than once really decent people misbehave because they thought they owed a loyalty to their CEO to deliver certain numbers. We want to keep people from misbehaving for ego satisfaction and for financial rewards.

---

[18] Henry Earl Singleton (November 27, 1916 – August 31, 1999) was an American electrical engineer, business executive, and rancher/landowner. He co-founded Teledyne, Inc. with George Kozmetsky and was CEO for three decades. For more, see *The Outsiders: Eight Unconventional CEOs and Their Radically Rational Blueprint for Success* by William N. Thorndike, Boston, MA: Harvard Business Review Press.

Charlie: At the end, Henry wanted to sell his business to Berkshire for stock. He was smart right to the end.

Warren: Jack Ringwalt[19] ran National Indemnity extremely well. Ringwalt's good friend and tennis partner at the firm was in charge of processing claims. When his friend would come into Jack's office to tell him he had received an insurance claim of $25,000, Jack would start berating the fellow by telling him the claims were killing him. Jack was joking, but the fellow started hiding the claims because he didn't want to face the tirades they caused. This caused the company to misreport its results. The fellow had no financial interest to misbehave, but he just didn't like Jack kidding him about failing him.

Managers need to be careful about the messages they send employees. If you tell your managers you never want to disappoint Wall Street, they start fudging figures. Berkshire tries to avoid all that.

Q22. Becky Quick: If government regulators deem Berkshire's reinsurance business as too big to fail, what impact would that have on Berkshire?

---

[19] Arthur and Jack Ringwalt, entrepreneurial brothers, founded National Indemnity Company in 1940 in a two-room office with four employees (including president Jack Ringwalt) in Omaha, Nebraska, as a specialty insurance firm that wrote liability insurance on taxis.

Warren: There are two regulatory aspects. European regulators look at insurers generally in terms of whether they are SIFI,[20] and they pay special attention to a group of about nine insurers. In the U.S., we have the Financial Stability Oversight Committee, which designates a financial institution as SIFI when 85 percent of revenues come from the financial side. They designated GE, Prudential, and MetLife as SIFI in addition to the big banks. At Berkshire, the revenue from financial operations is about 20 percent. We have no reason to think Berkshire Hathaway would be designated as a SIFI.

Size alone isn't the only criterion. ExxonMobil, Apple, Walmart are large. Nobody is questioning them why they are not designated as SIFI.

I think the real question is whether problems at Berkshire could destabilize the financial system in the country.

It's a moot question. The law exists, but we haven't been approached and we are miles away from being considered strategically important.

---

[20]Systemically Important Financial Institution (SIFI). There is no standard definition; however, the Basel Committee on Banking Supervision has identified factors for assessing whether a financial institution is systemically important, such as its size, complexity, interconnectedness, the lack of readily available substitutes for the financial infrastructure it provides, and its global (cross-jurisdictional) activity.

We conduct ourselves in a way that the activities of other financial institutions will not affect us.

During the last time of trouble we were about the only party supplying help to the financial system and we'll always conduct ourselves in a way that the problems of others can't hurt us in a significant way. I don't think Berkshire comes anywhere near a SIFI.

Charlie: I think there's a lot of risk in high finance, and the thought that Dodd-Frank did away with the risk is ridiculous. The idea of trading derivatives is like running a bucket shop or gambling parlor. You say you're sharing risk, and that's mostly nonsense— people just like making money with their gambling parlors. I think our competitors don't like it that they deserve regulation and we don't.

Warren: My understanding is that Dodd-Frank weakens the power of both the Fed and the Treasury to take actions like the ones they took in 2008, and I think those actions were downright necessary.

To have people believe you when you say "Whatever needs to be done will be done" is essential. That people believed Hank Paulson when he said money-market funds would be protected— that prevented a devastating run on money-market funds, which could have taken down the entire system.

When you have a panic, you have to have someone somewhere who can say and be correctly believed that he or she will do whatever it takes. You saw what happened when Draghi, Bernanke, and Paulson were able to say that. If they can't say that, panics will accelerate like you'd never believe. The only way they could get the job done was to make guarantees without exceptions. I think Dodd-Frank weakens that, and I think that's a bad thing.

Q23. Gary Ransom: GEICO is trying to sell workers' compensation insurance policies online. Do you see any channel conflict there? What is the future of online selling there?

Warren: We are not worried about undercutting our agents. We just want to see what the consumer wants. I don't think channel conflict between direct and agent-driven sales is a big problem for us.

We believe in experimenting at Berkshire and we believe we have the know-how. We will find out if the customers want to buy insurance that way.

The nature of the insurance business has changed significantly since Leo Goodman and his wife were stuffing envelopes in GEICO's early days in the 1930s. The world moves on and the key is to save people money and give them good service. GEICO has adapted to a lot of things over the years, from direct mail to TV/phone to cable TV and to the Internet. It helps people to save money. The basic idea of saving consumers' money continues till today.

It's now the number two car insurer in the U.S. We will stay at the top.

Q24. Shareholder, Station 8: After all these years of interviews and meetings, what is the one question you've never been asked that you'd like to answer now?

Warren: I think I've been asked almost all of them, and many questions time and time again.

Charlie, do you have anything you're dying to be asked?

Charlie: First, tell us the worst thing you ever did in your life.

Warren: Do you have a second question?

Shareholder: Can I buy you lunch?

Q25. Andrew Ross Sorkin: You take great pride in running the company in a deliberate way that respects the management in place. Are you saying that 3G's management method is congruent with yours? If they ran Berkshire, wouldn't there be a lot of layoffs?

Warren: No. There will be some companies they will change. I would say GEICO, with 33,000 employees, is run just as efficiently as 3G would run it.

We don't believe in having extra people around. The newspapers have cut back as revenues have kept shrinking. The idea of running a fat operation just because you're profitable is crazy.

Charlie: What's the worse thing you had ever done?

Warren: I closed other mills long before I closed the Berkshire mill.

We were trying to reduce our labor complement all the time just to stay afloat, and in the end it didn't save us. I don't want any of our operations to be run with excess people. I may not police it as closely as 3G would, but I don't like it any more than they do. Berkshire newspapers had to cut back employees and we had to cut back employees in the textile business in the early days of the company. Some Berkshire businesses may have more people than needed, but we don't believe in running fat operations. Berkshire's owner manual never endorses running a business at a loss to have excess people around.

You see our attitude on excess people most clearly in how we run the home office. We have only twenty-five people at the home office. Charlie has two people in Los Angeles including himself.

Charlie: We're getting by with practically nothing.

Q26. Gregg Warren: Follow-up on 3G Capital. Looking at your consumer staples holdings, do you see potential for more consolidation?

Warren: There will be consolidation in the future. Strong brands endure—like the ones General Foods had in the 80s and that are with Kraft today. Strong brands are really potent stuff.

Heinz ketchup is a great brand. You'll always have a fight between the retailer and the consumer brand. In the end, the retailer may want to shift to a private label (and those have been around forever in the soft-drink field—I remember getting a six-pack of Sam's Cola from Sam Walton when it first came out), but the brands are powerful, too. You have to build and enhance the brands. See's had to address the risk of competition from Russell Stover.[21] A strong brand will survive, and the great retailers will do well, too—but they'll always be in tension.

Charlie: We've almost exhausted this topic. There is no question about the fact that waves of layoffs frighten a lot of people. Jobs are a huge part of people's identities. But what would our country be if we'd kept all of our people on the farm milking cows? We need our businesses to be right-sized.

---

[21] Russell and Clara Stover founded a candy business in their home in Denver, Colorado, in 1923. In 1960, the company was purchased by Mr. Louis Ward. In 2014, Lindt & Sprungli, a worldwide manufacturer of premium-quality chocolates with roots back to the early 1800s, purchased Russell Stover Candies from the Ward Family. http://www.russellstover.com

Q27. Shareholder, Station 9: The Chinese capital market is almost double in the last few months. Do you think value investing can be widely applicable to all markets, including China?

Warren: Investment principles don't stop at borders. If I were investing in China, India, or the UK, I'd apply exactly the same principles I learned in *The Intelligent Investor*.[22] I'd look at stocks as small pieces of the business. I'd look at price fluctuations as a source of opportunity. I'd look for great businesses at good prices.

Charlie: Chinese people have a history of betting hard at times of good opportunity, and that makes things volatile. When things get bouncy, China can look a lot like Silicon Valley. They will do better if they do value.

Warren: We will do best in a market that people behave foolishly—exaggerating responses to events, getting wildly excited and wildly depressed—that's great for investors, but it's bad for society. We've benefitted enormously from irrational periods, most especially around 1974, when there were incredibly cheap opportunities. If you can behave like a young investor, evaluate stocks like businesses, and invest when things are very cheap (no matter what the people on TV say), you will do very well.

---

[22] The investment classic written by Benjamin Graham, Warren Buffett's professor at Columbia University.

Investment isn't a very tough intellectual game, if you take care of your emotions. China has more speculative forces than the U.S., which lends itself to greater extremes, but this should produce great opportunities.

Charlie: China is wise to dampen the speculative booms. Value investing will never go out of style. Who the hell doesn't want value when they're buying things? Why do we want it everywhere but in stocks?

Warren: Yet it's never very popular. Investors should buy businesses based on a long-term perspective. No one should buy a farm thinking they are going to make money on it the next week.

Q28. Carol Loomis: You have expressed your optimism for the U.S. economy. My question concerns risks from chemical, nuclear, biological, and cyber ("CNBC") threats. How do these threats put America at risk?

Warren: The economic system is enormously powerful. There will be fits and starts, but imagine what a flyover tour of the country would have looked like in 1776. Everything that's been developed since that time is profit. People fret about a 2 percent economic growth rate, but with a 1 percent population growth rate, that still results in major growth over time. But great growth can be negated by the work of madmen, sociopaths, and religious fanatics who wish to have access to weapons of mass destruction. We already have a huge number of people that wish harm on the U.S. who will look for more ingenious ways to hurt our system. They will not go away. We need an extremely vigilant security operation in the U.S. The country will do extraordinarily well if we ward off those threats or at least minimize their impact. The luckiest person in history on a probabilistic basis is the baby born in the U.S. today.

Charlie: I think I've lived in the most ideal period of human history. But we shouldn't get too smug. We have been lucky too. China has come along, too—faster than any other nation in history.

Warren: And that's good for us.

Charlie: I can't think of anything more important than future close collaboration between the U.S. and China. I think it's enormously important that we like and trust each other. Both countries would be crazy not to collaborate and increase trust. There's nothing more important that we could do for our safety or for the general benefit of the world.

Warren: Would you rather be born today or when you were born?

Charlie: It's very interesting now, but it's always been interesting. I don't like theoretical questions like this. I'd rather think about questions where I can either gain an advantage or help someone else gain an advantage.

Q29. Jonathan Brandt: It is your assertion in the past that Berkshire in the future will have a CEO and a CIO (Chief Investment Officer). Do these positions need to be mutually exclusive?

Warren: Good question. It is very unlikely but not inconceivable that they could be the same person. The CIO should have the skills that are useful for a CEO too. I would not want to put someone whose sole experience is in investments in charge of Berkshire if they didn't have significant operating experience. I've always said I'm a better investor because I've been a better operator.

I've seen a lot of businesses run by people who didn't understand the financial and investing background. Some of our operating managers know a lot about investing.

Charlie: Operating companies have become more and more important at Berkshire. So we need people who have both experiences. Having a dual background is useful.

Warren: The CEO needs to have an understanding of investing and capital allocation.

Q30. Shareholder, Station 10: What is Ted Weschler's investment philosophy?

Warren: Both Ted and Todd are very smart about businesses as well as investment. They understand reality and know competitive strengths. On top of that they have qualities that both Charlie and I really like.

We've seen people self-destruct in pursuit of making money they didn't really need because they were already rich.

When I closed my partnership, I asked my partners to contact Bill Ruane of Sequoia Fund. If you invested $10,000 with him, you would have $4 million now. He was a great investment manager and also a terrific human being.

A good manager will not take credit for work that he didn't do. Ted and Todd fit that bill. Charlie met Todd first and I met Ted. We talked about their investment performance, but we talked a lot more about what type of people they are and we've been very pleased.

Charlie: The whole thing with Ted and Todd has worked out really well. Each one helped buy a business recently and helped to run them too. They are smart, they have good business sense, and they know how to handle people.

Warren: They will help us oversee businesses. Todd was involved in the Phillips 66 deal[23] and Ted with

---

[23] Phillips 66 (NYSE: PSX) is an American multinational energy company headquartered in Westchase, Houston, Texas. In 2013, for $1.4 billion, Berkshire bought Phillips Specialty Products, a wholly owned subsidiary of Phillips 66, which develops polymers that improve the flow of oil through pipelines.

the recent German acquisition. Charlie and I have run into more dysfunctional people with 160 IQs than most people. A lot of people are incapable of functioning well day after day even though they're capable of brilliance from time to time.

Charlie: Trustworthiness is more important than the brain. We wouldn't hire anybody, no matter how able they were, if we didn't trust them.

Warren: We are approaching noon.

I want to give a brief update about my bet with the hedge fund of funds.

[Background: this is a bet between Warren Buffett and Protégé Partners, a New York City money management company. The bet is that, according to Warren, over a ten-year period a passive investment in the market index (S&P 500) will yield better returns to the investor than the (after-fees) returns from a carefully selected portfolio of hedge funds supposedly managed by some of the best investment minds in the world.]

Warren: Our market vs. hedge fund bet is now seven years old. Even after a rough start in 2008, the market is up by 63.5 percent and the fund of hedge funds 19 percent. Last year, the market returned 13.6 percent and the fund of hedge funds returned 5.6 percent.

We bought Vanguard market index fund. With their fees, the hedge funds have done well; it's their investors who have paid the price of their underperformance.

You can track the bet here:[24]
http://longbets.org/362/

... Recess ...

[24] See also
http://archive.fortune.com/2008/06/04/news/newsmakers/buff
ett_bet.fortune/index.htm

Questions and Answers: Part 2

"Develop yourself into the person you admire the most. The good thing is that you will be stuck with yourself for the rest of your life."
Warren Buffett

"Nothing beats behaving well as you go through life."
Charlie Munger

"Companies should use their capital to take care of their business needs and only repurchase their stock when the price is trading substantially below intrinsic value."
Warren Buffett

"When you're older and aren't deteriorating as fast as your contemporaries, you may pay more for auto insurance, but that may be a worthwhile trade-off."
Charlie Munger

Warren: If you can find your seats, we'll get started. I'll give you another minute or two to settle down.

Q31. Becky Quick: Which of Berkshire businesses would suffer the most in a period of high inflation and why?

Warren: The best investments during inflation are the ones you can buy once without having to buy into them again over and over. That's why real estate can be good in an inflationary period. If you built your house fifty years ago like Charlie and I did, it's a one-time outlay. You then get an inflationary expansion in value.

If you are in the utility or railroad business, or any business with heavy capital investment, then you are stuck with capital replacement year after year. These are poor businesses in an inflationary environment.

Value of brands is also valuable during inflation. If you have a brand, the value increases over time. We've had to nourish the See's brand over time, but the value of the brand increased along with inflation. Gillette bought the radio rights to the 1939 World Series; think of the number of impressions they got then for $100,000. Millions of people got the impressions in those dollars. If you tried to get the same thing today, it would cost you vastly more. It was a great investment that could be made in 1939 dollars that paid off still in 1960, 1970, and 1980 dollars.

Charlie: If inflation goes out of control, you have no idea where you are going to end up. Inflation in the Weimer Republic Germany brought us Hitler. We don't want inflation just because it's good for See's Candies.

Q32. Gary Ransom: Has Berkshire Hathaway Specialty Insurance been doing well enough that they don't need to make an acquisition?

Warren: It is almost 100 percent certain that we'll not take on a large commercial operation—just too big of an acquisition premium. We have a good operation, great managers, and more capital than everyone else. If we acquired an outsider, we'd have to pay a substantial control premium. There's almost zero probability that we'll buy another commercial insurance company.

BH Specialty Insurance could become a big operation five to ten years from now.

Charlie: I certainly agree with you.

Warren: Trying to keep your job.

Q33. Shareholder, Station 11: What practical mental model or models would you impress on a young, enterprising individual to build an important enterprise with a similar impact as Berkshire or Microsoft?

Charlie: Reputation is earned over a long period of time. Very few people are like Charles Lindbergh[25] and gain one instantly. You have to build the reputation you can in the time available to you. It's a wise investment. I see opportunities all the time that arise for people who took advantage of previous opportunities. Nothing beats behaving well as you go through life. We have tried to behave better as we've gotten more prosperous. I don't think there's any way of guaranteeing a powerhouse brand, nor achieving great success with low odds.

Warren: The former chairman of Fiat once told me, "Whatever reputation you have when you get old, it's probably the one you deserve." It is what you have developed over time. Berkshire has benefited from its strong reputation, which wasn't necessarily the end goal. The same is true for companies.

Q34. Andrew Ross Sorkin: You have maintained that global warming hasn't affected Berkshire's insurance pricing, whereas other insurers say otherwise. Travelers[26] also consider this as a risk. Could you please explain?

---

[25] An American aviator, author, inventor, military officer, explorer, and social activist who operated the first solo nonstop transatlantic airplane flight in 1927.

[26] Travelers Companies, Inc. (NYSE: TRV) is an American insurance company, headquartered in New York. It is the second-largest writer of U.S. commercial property and casualty insurance and the third-largest writer of U.S. personal insurance through independent agents.

Warren: SEC requires us to put all these risk factors in the reports. And the lawyers will say the same. They want us to put it [climate change] in because some models have found it relevant.

In the case of property and casualty insurance (more than life insurance), I see nothing that tells me that on a yearly basis global warming should cause me to change my prices a lot. The insurer can adjust pricing every year based on changing conditions.

It would be different if I am writing a fifty-year coverage for hurricane in Florida or Louisiana. I will be more careful. So it's not something I put in the 10-K as a threat.

Charlie: I don't think it's clear what the results will be over the extremes in weather. There are a lot of people who howl a lot about potential calamities. A lot of people get invested in things and act like they would under the influence of an extreme ideology. That doesn't mean global warming isn't happening and isn't important, but it's easy to take it too far.

Warren: Will it change your policy?

Charlie: No.

Warren: Not mine, either.

Charlie: It's crazy.

Warren: So if you ask me, will we change pricing in one year? No. In fifty years? Probably yes.

I don't want my underwriters thinking about global warming; I want them to be looking at the moral hazard of the person owning the property. If you're insuring Marvin the Torch,[27] global warming doesn't matter. Marvin said, "I don't burn buildings; I create vacant lots."

Q35. Gregg Warren: Given your bad experience with ConocoPhillips in the past, you took a meaningful position in ExxonMobil in 2013. Why not let Berkshire Energy do these deals?

Warren: BH Energy is really in a dramatically different industry than ExxonMobil or ConocoPhillips. We wrote ConocoPhillips down because we were required to by the auditors. We actually made some money on it.

There's nothing we like better than BH Energy. We call it energy but it's not oil and gas. We believe BH Energy will continue to seek acquisition opportunities in the utility industry.

My ambition ever since buying MidAmerican in 1995 is to get it to the point where it earns $35.05 a

---

[27] Marvin the Torch never could keep his hands off somebody else's business, particularly if the business was losing money. Now this is accepted behavior in Marvin's profession, which is arson. http://www.nytimes.com/2004/11/14/nyregion/thecity/14bres.html?_r=0

share, which is the price we paid. I didn't change my offer prices. They continued to negotiate hard and said you have to give us something. I agreed to pay $35.05 per share and told them they could say they got the last nickel out of me. It'll probably earn about $30 a share this year, even though it doesn't pay a dividend. We've made a little money there, but we've not distinguished ourselves.

We don't buy oil and gas very often, but we will likely buy some. There's nothing we like better than backing up Greg [Abel] and his people in buying energy properties.

Strong management team, strong growth prospects, and constructive regulatory jurisdictions are key attributes we highlight for future acquisitions. The recently acquired NV Energy and AltaLink meet all these requirements in our opinion.

Charlie: With interest rates so low and dividends on ExxonMobil being what they were, it was not a bad cash substitution.

Q36. Station 1, New York: Our tax code is broken. $2.2 or $2.1 trillion cash is sitting outside of the U.S. What can be done to bring about a simpler or more rational tax code?

Warren: It takes 218 members of the House of Representatives and 51 senators, plus a president who will sign the bill. Despite complaints from executives, corporations have expanded their share of the national income while decreasing their share of tax payments. Absent a major revision of the tax code, it's difficult to extract special exceptions from the tax code. If we're going to spend 21 percent of GDP, we need to raise 19 percent of GDP in taxes. We can run a 2–3 percent deficit. However, if you take 19 percent of a $17.5 trillion economy, you're talking real money. How much you get from where is a fight up the line.

In terms of cash parked abroad, companies can bring it back to the U.S., but they will have to pay the corporate tax rate on it. I think there can be a much more equitable tax code in terms of corporate tax. However, I don't shed tears on the current corporate tax rate as American businesses are still prospering. Our corporate rates are 35 percent; we used to deal with them at 52 percent and at 48 percent, and the country grew at those times. Paying 2 percent of GDP is not an onerous number when corporations are earning 15 percent on tangible equity. Equity holders are being treated well, especially in comparison to savers who are only getting $\frac{1}{4}$ percent or $\frac{1}{2}$ percent on CDs.

Charlie: I live in California, where there is a 13.5 percent tax on capital gains. That's ridiculous, as it is driving rich people out of California. Hawaii and Florida understand that seniors don't create a lot of crime and they don't use services like schools; meanwhile they spend a lot of money on things like health care, so they're very attractive.

Warren: Early stage of paranoia.

Charlie: The idea of driving out the rich people makes Florida seem vastly smarter than California. California looks demented. Who the hell doesn't want rich people coming into their state and spending money? I think California has a stupid tax policy, but I don't think the federal tax policy is bad at all.

Warren: Remember that when you come to Nebraska for the meeting. I credit Ron Wyden[28] and Orrin Hatch.[29] Two people are capable of working out something that neither of them likes very well, but that will work. What would have happened at the Constitutional Convention in Philadelphia[30] if the delegates had been running out to give TV interviews after every debate? I don't think it's impossible to imagine having a new corporate tax code within the next year.

Q37. Carol Loomis: When asked, you always talk about four books—three by Benjamin

---

[28] Ronald Lee "Ron" Wyden is the senior United States senator for Oregon, serving since 1996, and a member of the Democratic Party.

[29] Orrin Grant Hatch is an American politician who is the president pro tempore of the United States Senate, serving since January 2015. A member of the Republican Party, he serves as the senior U.S. senator for Utah.

[30] The Constitutional Convention in Philadelphia met between May and September 1787 to address the problems of the weak central government that existed under the Articles of Confederation. After the necessary number of state ratifications, the Constitution came into effect in 1789 and has served as the basis of the United States government ever since.
https://history.state.gov/milestones/1784-1800/convention-and-ratification

Graham and the other, *The Wealth of Nations*, by Adam Smith. What did you learn from *The Wealth of Nations* and how did it shape your investment and business thinking?

Warren: It didn't shape my investment philosophies. I certainly learned economics from it.

I got my original copy from Bill Gates. If you read Adam Smith, Keynes, Ricardo, or *Where Are the Customers' Yachts?*,[31] you will have a lot of wisdom. That book [*Where Are the Customers' Yachts?*] contains an incredible amount of wisdom in a short number of pages.

Charlie?

Charlie: Adam Smith is one of those guys that have really worn well. He is among the wisest people that ever came along. He demonstrated the productive power of the capitalist system. And you can see why communism failed so spectacularly.

Warren: The idea is that you let other people do what they're best at and you do what you're best at. I took Smith's ideas of division of labor and applied them to mowing my lawn as well as to my philanthropy.

---

[31] *Where Are the Customers' Yachts? or A Good Hard Look at Wall Street* by Fred Schwed, Jr. New York: Wiley.

Charlie: You don't do your own bowel surgery, either.

Q38. Jonathan Brandt: Do managements at Berkshire's formerly public companies have earnings-management behavior that carries over from their public days? Is there more that can be done to combat that behavior?

Warren: If we match public vs. private companies, I can't tell which delivered better value. I don't think we've had problems with public vs. private companies we've bought.

Charlie: I don't know where you get this idea that earnings management is taking place. It's not apparent to us.

Warren: No real problems come to mind. Our managers certainly know how to run Berkshire for the next hundred years. We tell them we think about hundred years out, and they know we mean that. I think we set the right example, and I think we use words to convey that belief as strongly as we can. It is evidenced in our annual reports. We believe in hammering the same message over and over again.

Not to say they ignore annual results, of course. I don't think they're unimportant, but we don't live by them. What matters is where we will be three, five, and ten years from now. If we're working to maximize returns over ten years, that doesn't mean we're out to throw away money.

Q39. Shareholder, Station 2: What differences in corporate culture do you see between German and U.S. companies?

Warren: I am looking for some good German companies.

Charlie: We had a hard time buying things in Europe. That's been quite rare. The family traditions in Europe are different from what they are in the U.S. Germany, of course, has a very long tradition of being good at technology and capitalism. And we admire the Germans, particularly the engineers. They actually work fewer hours than American but they produce a lot more. Of course, Warren and I are very good at that.

Warren: I will make one prediction. We will buy one German company within the next five years. I would really be surprised if we don't make another deal in Germany in the next five years. We hope Mrs. Louis's contact will contact us again with some acquisition ideas. I've got four or five letters but they are all small businesses. We're eager, we have the money, and we do fit the family situation occasionally. Prices may be a little more attractive there than in the U.S.

Q40. Becky Quick: The questioner asked that he and his wife are in their 70s, have clean driving records, but didn't get a quote from GEICO that improved upon the rates they pay now.

Warren: We beat other companies 40 percent of the time, and 60 percent of the time we can't. We have 11 percent of the market now, so we should have a lot of room for additional growth. We know that sixteen-year-old boys are as bad as you will get to insure; sixteen-year-old girls don't tend to show off, they're a better class. We have to ask a lot of questions to do our underwriting.

Every company has its underwriting criteria. We have our own underwriting criteria, which has many variables. Age is one of them. Different firms weight different variables differently.

GEICO considers a list of variables in underwriting. So it can't offer the lowest price 100 percent of the time. But I don't think any company of that size will offer the low price more often than GEICO.

We give quotes over the phone every week. It's definitely worth fifteen minutes to call GEICO.

Charlie: When you're older and aren't deteriorating as fast as your contemporaries, you may pay more for auto insurance, but that may be a worthwhile trade-off.

"I was pretty obnoxious when I was your age, [7th grade] and asked a lot of impertinent questions. Not everybody liked me. The only way I could get people to like me was to get very rich and very generous."
Charlie Munger

"There's no Forbes 400 in the graveyard."
Charlie Munger

"Everybody should have his or her own philosophy [for philanthropy]. I could buy ten houses or a hotel. But that won't make me any happier."
Warren Buffett

"Praise by name, criticize by category."
Warren Buffett

Q41. Gary Ransom: The reinsurance market has changed a lot recently. What are you and Ajit doing to take advantage of the next opportunity?

Warren: Wouldn't our competitors like to know? Reinsurance business is not as good as it used to be. A lot of money has come into the market not because people are seeking to reinsure wisely but because it's a way to break out earnings. It's possible to set up a hedge fund in Bermuda under cover of starting a reinsurance business, and some parties will use that reinsurance business as a "beard" to avoid taxes in the hedge fund. With that going on, they'll sometimes buy reinsurance business just to make it look like they're legitimate. It's hard to compete with them.

Reinsurance business will not be as good in the future as it was thirty years ago. There is nothing you can do about it. It's a business whose prospects have turned for the worse.

Charlie: These parties getting into reinsurance for asset diversification are searching for a strong narrative. We're not searching for a narrative. We don't particularly like the way the reinsurance game is being played.

Q42: Station 3, 7th grade student from Florida: How do you make friends and get people to work with you?

Warren: Good question.

Charlie: I was pretty obnoxious when I was your age, and asked a lot of impertinent questions. Not everybody liked me. The only way I could get people to like me was to get very rich and very generous.

Warren: Both Charlie and I were on the obnoxious side when we were younger. I have learned to become a better person with age.

If I admire someone, why wouldn't I want to take on their better qualities? If you look around at the people you like in your school, write down what you like about them, and do the same for the bad qualities of people that turn you off.

First Ben Graham did this and then I thought it was a good example for me to follow. Ben Graham said to take a sheet of paper and list all the qualities you admire in people on one side and the things you don't like on the other side. He did that and realized that the list of things he admired were not traits that were out of reach. They were all things he could learn and practice, so he did it. Similarly, he figured that the things he didn't like about people and himself were not things you have to be stuck with for life. You can train yourself to get rid of those undesirable traits.

I will advise you to do this for yourself and develop yourself into the person you admire the most. The good thing is that you will be stuck with yourself for the rest of your life.

Charlie: That really works in marriage. You can change yourself easier than you can change your spouse.

Warren: According to Charlie, when looking for a marriage partner, don't look for intelligence, humor, or character; look for someone with very low expectations.

Q43. Andrew Ross Sorkin: This question is about the labor unrest at NetJets, which produced a picket line of pilots outside the CenturyLink Center all day. Any comment on the NetJets pilot strike? Was buying NetJets a mistake?

Warren: Buying NetJets was not a mistake. NetJets is a very good business. ROI[32] isn't the best way to look at it. We sell those planes to others; they are owners. I have flown NetJets for twenty years. I own $^3/_8$ and my children own $^3/_{16}$.

In fifty years we've had three strikes that I can remember—four-day strike each at Berkshire Hathaway textile, See's Candies, and *Buffalo News*.

The NetJets employees have good jobs. We don't have any anti-union agenda whatsoever. We think we have nothing but professional pilots. On average we pay $145,000 per year. Pilots have many

---

[32] Return on investment, measures the amount of return on an investment relative to the cost of investment. It's a very popular comparison measure because of its simplicity, sometimes it may lead to misleading decisions.

options and they work the "seven days on, seven days off" model. We pay them well.

Compared to our competitors, we are doing much better. Our volume is up in terms of hours and in terms of owners. It's a first-class operation that is focused on safety and we give our pilots more training than other companies.

It's perfectly understandable that employees and employers will have differences from time to time. At the moment, we've got a difference of opinion about a contract and we will work it out.

Charlie: I'm not sure the union is fairly representing these fellows. I have never seen any NetJets pilot say they are unhappy.

Warren: He said fellows, but we have women pilots as well.

Q44. Gregg Warren: Looking at Duracell, it's a business in decline, even if it is creating cash flow. How much of a role did taxes play in the deal? Would you have done this deal without tax considerations?

Warren: Both P&G and Berkshire have tax advantages in this deal. Neither party would have done the deal without the tax advantages. We didn't get net tax break.

Berkshire held stocks in P&G for over five years. The exchange is somewhat similar to Section 1031 of real estate exchange agreement[33] where you can exchange it and defer taxes a little bit. There wouldn't have been a transaction if it wasn't for the fact of the exchange arrangement.

Battery business is a declining business, but it's not about to disappear. I look forward to getting the purchase completed, probably by the fourth quarter. P&G has been fun to work with. I will be very happy to work with them.

Q45. Station 4, Texas: At the annual meeting a couple of years ago, I asked you about estate planning and you advised me to leave kids with enough that they could do anything, but not so much that they wouldn't do anything. What prompted you to sign the giving pledge and why are you giving away at least half of your fortune? What is your view on philanthropies?

Warren: Actually, I've promised to give over 99 percent of my wealth to philanthropy. It's a very individual thing. As you know, the estate tax exemption has been moved up substantially, so I might have a very different feeling if I'd had a child who worked very actively to help me build this, and it was a small business that I wanted to give to him.

---

[33] http://www.irs.gov/uac/Like-Kind-Exchanges-Under-IRC-Code-Section-1031

If I am running a small business, then estate tax will matter.

The options get fairly limited when it comes to figuring out what to do with your money. The question is, where does it do the most good? Stock certificates in a safety deposit box do me no good. It adds nothing to my happiness, no utility at all to me. They have enormous use in other parts of the world, so why in the world should they sit there for me or for some fourth generation of great-grandchildren when they can do good elsewhere?

As Charlie has said, "There's no Forbes 400 in the graveyard." Old stock certificates can't help me to consume 7,000 calories instead of 2,000, but they can do a lot of good for other people. I want to get the most utility out of my resources. When someone tells me that he's seventy and doesn't want to think about his assets yet, I ask him whether he's going to make a better decision at age ninety-five with a blonde in his lap.

The question is where does it do the most amount of good. Everybody should have his or her own philosophy.

I could buy ten houses or a hotel. But that won't make me any happier.

Charlie: When the politicians changed the rules to increase the estate tax exemption to $5 million, it was a very constructive change in the law. I don't think we should assume that our politicians are always going to be totally crazy.

Q46. Carol Loomis: Would it make sense for Berkshire to distribute at some time in the future any or some of the long-term equity investments like Coca-Cola or AMEX to shareholders? Should Berkshire do the same with appreciated securities what Yahoo! Inc. did with its Alibaba stake?

Charlie: There is no way to do that.

Warren: You would have to pay full capital gains tax to do it.

Charlie: It's a bad example.

Warren: What Yahoo is trying to do, they will not get rid of taxes. I know all kinds of cases where people got shares without the company paying tax at the corporate level.

Q47. Jonathan Brandt: You said earlier that more young people would stay with their parents. Jobs are now plentiful yet the housing market is still sluggish. Will the U.S. become more like Europe where children live with parents longer? Or is this a cyclical phenomenon?

Warren: I don't know the answer to this question. The latter is more likely. I would expect it to turn up but I don't know. But I suspect that young people will want to have their own homes again. I did a good job selling the ring to this young couple.[34] I hope they will be buying a home soon.

It always turns down in a recession, and you can argue that the recession isn't over yet.

Charlie: I have some grandchildren that I wish would marry somebody suitable promptly. They should quit looking for pie in the sky or whatever the hell they're doing. I don't want to name names.

Q48. Shareholder, Station 5, Omaha: I have a son in Indonesia working with the poor. What could Berkshire shareholders do philanthropically to improve the lives of non-shareholders?

Warren: I really feel I've got everything I need, but I also feel I'm working for the shareholders but they should determine their own philanthropic activities. I believe in individual philanthropy rather than corporate philanthropy. I encourage our managers to do so. I don't want to write a check from the company to my alma mater. This is not my money.

I've never given away a dollar that had any marginal utility to me. I admire those who give away money that could have made their own lives better.

---

[34] Warren Buffett helped a Berkshire Hathaway shareholder to propose to his girlfriend at Borsheim's Jewelry during the 2014 Berkshire annual shareholders meeting. https://youtu.be/yTHy4W-qDYY

Charlie?

Charlie: My taste for giving away other people's money is also quite restrained.

Warren: I have real reservations about corporate philanthropy for that reason.

Q49. Becky Quick: Euro as a currency did some good things but at the same time it faced some challenges. What do you think about the future of that?

Warren: It is too easy for me to answer so I'll give it to Charlie.

Charlie: I don't have the faintest idea. The euro had a noble motivation and it has undoubtedly done a lot of good things. But it's a flawed system in some ways to put countries that are so different together. There are countries in the Eurozone that shouldn't be there. The big problem is Greece and Portugal.

You can't form a business partnership with your frivolous, drunken brother-in-law. I think they lowered their standards a little and it's caused strains.

Warren: Everything here is off the record.

Everything humans make contains flaws, including our own Constitution. Just because something wasn't perfectly designed at first doesn't mean it should be abandoned. We could have had a common currency with Canada and we could have made it work.

I think North America (U.S. and Canada) should have a common currency, but not all the countries of the Western hemisphere should be included.

Charlie: Like Argentina?

Warren: Praise by name, criticize by category [one of Warren Buffett's pet philosophies – praises people individually by name but criticizes the type of activity he doesn't like that people are involved in rather than the people]. It's probably desirable to have a euro currency designed and enforced so that the rules really apply. There were rules on the euro that were broken early on by the Germans and the French.

Charlie: Investment bankers helped them prepare phony financial statements. It was investment-banker-aided fraud, not exactly noble.

Warren: The euro can and will survive. It needs more cohesion. In its present form, it is probably not going to work.

Charlie? I don't know why I am giving you another shot?

Charlie: I think I've offended enough people.

Q50. Gary Ransom: Are there synergies between GEICO and Van Tuyl in selling car insurance?

Warren: I don't think it is a good idea. Those two companies will do better if they are run as independent businesses. Investment bankers will say synergy, but it doesn't work. Historically, selling auto insurance through dealerships hasn't been that effective.

We would have to compensate the dealers to sell the insurance and that adds costs. GEICO thrives because it is low-cost. Tony Nicely did a good job there.

Charlie: I agree. It's a very dumb idea and we are not going to do it.

"I can't think of many activists I would want to marry into my family."
Charlie Munger

"It is important to start good habits early. ... I was $9,000 or $10,000 ahead of my classmates when I got out of school. ... My life could have turned out very differently without that head start."
Warren Buffett

"A lot is taught in higher education that isn't very useful, and a lot of people there don't learn much of anything."
Charlie Munger

"If you're enjoying what you're doing, you're likely to get better results than if you go to work with your teeth clenched every morning."
Warren Buffett

"The people who follow the Graham-Newman model have all done well. If you can avoid being a perfect idiot, you can do very well."
Charlie Munger

Q51. Shareholder, Station 6: Do you see value in silver?

Warren: I don't think so. Silver is a by-product of copper. I bought $100 million ounces of silver once. It's a very small market. We don't think about silver anymore.

Charlie: It's a pretty good thing, too. We didn't do too well in it.

Warren: We came out better than the Hunt brothers,[35] but we don't think about it much anymore.

Q52. Andrew Ross Sorkin: Charlie said in the past he saw activism getting worse before it gets better. If Warren is giving his shares away to charities over a term, what if activists interfere? Would you think that the parts are worth more than the whole?

Warren: It's unlikely that the value of the parts will be greater than the value of the total. It might look like it, but that wouldn't be the case. There are a lot of benefits to having the company as one with one corporate tax return. I think it's unlikely that, on any long-term or intermediate basis, the value of the parts is greater than the value of the whole.

Activism is increasing because it's easy for

---

[35] Nelson Bunker Hunt and William Herbert Hunt, the sons of Texas oil billionaire Haroldson Lafayette Hunt, Jr., attempted to corner the silver market in the 1980s by taking substantial positions in the futures market.

them to raise money. The best defense against activism is performance. Lately, with so much money poured into activist funds, it has been a successful way of getting money to flow.

If you're talking about my shares getting dispensed ten years after my estate's settled, I think by the time that's a reality, Berkshire's value will be so great that activists won't be able to do much about it. People are very worried about activist investors. We say we will welcome them.

Charlie: There is more stupid stuff written and done by activists like urging companies to repurchase their shares when the price is greater than the value. If you have a partnership, and the partner wants to sell out to you at 120 percent of what it's worth, you wouldn't do it. However, if you look at the history of share repurchases, the activity falls off when stocks are cheap.

Warren: Companies should use their capital to take care of their business needs and only repurchase their stock when the price is trading substantially below intrinsic value. If Berkshire were to trade at 1.2 times book value, Berkshire will buy back bushel baskets of Berkshire stock, but not at 2.0 times book value, as it would not be worth that price.

Charlie: I can't think of many activists I would want to marry into my family.

Warren: I better stop before he names name.

Q53. Gregg Warren: American Express is the third largest holding of Berkshire. But competitors have been chipping away and Costco walked away from the relationship. How does AMEX protect its moat?

Warren: American Express is a very special company. Ken Chennault[36] has done a great job with the company. There's a lot of loyalty with AMEX cardholders. We are very happy with American Express. But we'll like it better if the price goes down and they buy back shares.

American Express is pretty good at innovation and technology. All payment providers are under pressure. American Express is aware of all of these issues. When there is more competition, companies with loyal customers will do better.

I'd better let the Costco director sitting here address this. Charlie?

Charlie: I liked it better when they had a little less competition, but that's life.

Warren: American Express has an incredible history of adapting. It started as an express mail company in 1850. They became very good at handling money.

---

[36] Kenneth Irvine Chenault is an American business executive. He has been the CEO and Chairman of American Express (NYSE: AXP) since 2001.

The company did wonders for Berkshire back in the 1960s. You feel like more important when you pull out your American Express card from your wallet. They are very nimble and very smart in terms of meeting challenges. I am delighted we own 15 percent of the company.

Q54. Station 7, Los Angeles: I've travelled a lot. Students in developing countries don't know much about money. I would like to teach financial literacy to South Americans. How do I do that?

Charlie: I failed in this endeavor with my relatives. I don't know if I can help you with that.

Warren: It is important to start good habits early. Samuel Johnson once said, "The chains of habit are too weak to be felt until they are too strong to be broken." Teach your children well early on. It can be life-changing. Young people can watch *The Secret Millionaires Club* cartoon.[37] I was $9,000 or $10,000 ahead of my classmates when I got out of school, and that helped me start a family right away. My life could have turned out very differently without that head start.

---

[37] *The Secret Millionaires Club* is an animated series that features Warren Buffett as a mentor to a group of entrepreneurial kids whose adventures lead them to encounter financial and business problems to solve. The program teaches the basics of good financial decision making and some of the basic lessons of starting a business. http://www.smckids.com

Q55. Station 8: Should Berkshire use cash to close out puts or get rid of other debt?

Warren: You are talking about equity put. We like to have the cash to be opportunistic. We virtually have no debt so there isn't much to pay off. Excess cash is cash above $20 billion. We have a policy of having more than $20 billion of cash. We will get calls and we will put more money to work.

If someone told us fifty years ago that we'd be able to borrow euros for a long duration at 1 percent, we'd have ended up with a far different balance sheet. Cheap money makes people do strange things on the asset side of the balance sheet. We don't want to go crazy on the liabilities side.

We don't want to drop our standards too fast only because the cost of borrowing is so low. We are not going to deleverage Berkshire because it is not highly leveraged to begin with. I see no drain on funds of any consequence from the float for as far as the eye can see. Technically, we can take on more debt but it is not something we like to do.

Charlie: We'll like something to come up that will stretch our capital capability. We haven't felt capital-constrained for a long time. It's a problem we'd love to have.

Q56. Station 9, China: There is a lack of economies of scale in auto dealerships in China. Does the rate of return on capital justify buying

more dealerships? What is the difference between U.S. and Chinese auto dealers?

Warren: I don't know the dealership situation in China. We aren't going to get significant benefits of scale in our auto dealership business. We need managers who have "skin in the game."

There are 71,000 dealerships, and we've got eighty-one of them, so there is a lot of room to grow. I don't know how we will do in China.

Charlie: I don't know. Van Tuyl will do better here.

Warren: We paid a full but fair price for Van Tuyl; we'll use that price as a yardstick for future purchases. We're having a big car year, and profits are good. If profits are good, we want to pay a lower multiple—we'd rather pay ten or twelve times the multiple of a bad year than eight times a good year.

Q57. Station 10, China: What's your secret to staying so energetic? Please don't say because of Coca-Cola. Will we keep doing more things on the Internet in the future?

Charlie: Warren is a big Internet user compared to me.

Warren: I spend $1 million per year for planes but only $100 for the Internet. If I had to give up one, I'd give up the plane.

Charlie: Interesting.

Warren: Charlie has given up both.

Charlie: Like it or not, we're living in a modern reality. The Internet is growing in importance, so like it or not, we're being dragged into it.

Warren: Sounds like you don't like it.

Charlie: I don't like multitasking. I have to think for such a long time to do anything that the idea of multitasking has never occurred to me.

It's amazing to me how dramatically the Internet has changed our lives in the last twenty to twenty-five years, and the game is not over yet. More people will use the Internet in the future. It changes our business at GEICO.

Warren: People get pessimistic about America, but just look at the Internet over the last twenty years. I try to imagine rounding up three of my buddies to play bridge on a snowy day. But with the Internet … and it's hard not to see the world as getting better.

Charlie: I'm partner.

Q58. Station 11: How concerned are you about income inequality? Do you support raising the minimum wage?

Warren: I think income inequality is extraordinary in the U.S. Since I was born in 1930, the average GDP in the U.S. went up six times. My parents thought they were living in a reasonably decent economy in 1930. If they'd known that it would go from $8,000 to $9,000 to $54,000, they would have thought everyone in America would be living a terrific life, but they're not.

I do think that everyone who is willing to work should have a reasonably decent livelihood in the U.S.

I have nothing against raising the minimum wage, but to raise it enough to make a difference would change the opportunities available to people very dramatically. I have plans to write something on the subject soon.[38]

I'm much more a believer in reforming and changing the Earned Income Tax Credit,[39] which rewards those who work but also helps those whose skills don't necessarily fit well in a particular job market.

---

[38] Warren Buffett wrote an article, "Better Than Raising the Minimum Wage," in the *Wall Street Journal* on May 21, 2015. http://www.wsj.com/articles/better-than-raising-the-minimum-wage-1432249927

[39] A benefit for working people who have low-to-moderate income. It is a tax credit, which reduces the amount of tax you owe and may also give you a refund. http://www.irs.gov/Credits-&-Deductions/Individuals/Earned-Income-Tax-Credit/EITC

Charlie: You've just heard a Democrat speaking. I think raising the minimum wage dramatically would be stupid and would hurt the poor.

Q59. Station 1, New York: Higher education is getting expensive day by day. Some schools cost about $60,000 a year [sticker price between $40,000 and $70,000]. How will the average American family be able to pay for college?

Charlie: The average American family affords it by going to less expensive places and getting massive subsidies. I think it is a big problem that the price of higher education keeps going up.

College-educated people do better, but maybe they do better because they were better to start with [implying their earnings are due to the personality and character, not because they are college graduates].

Warren: I think it's ridiculous to say that college education is worth X because that's the amount that people who go to college earn beyond what others do. You're only looking at one variable.

Charlie: As long as it works, they'll keep raising the prices. That's pretty much the way the system works.

A lot is taught in higher education that isn't very useful, and a lot of people there don't learn much of anything. When the great recession came, all of the colleges discovered they were overstaffed. They acted like 3G and laid off a bunch of staff. Now they're right-sized, and it works a lot better. Without some big incentive, I think higher education will keep raising its prices.

Q60. Station 2, China: What advice would you give on the Chinese economy?

Warren: China will do very fine over a period of time. Charlie is the China expert.

Charlie: I'm a big fan of what's happening in China. I've just ordered a bust of Lee Kuan Yew[40] because I think he contributed so much to fixing Singapore. One of the things he did was clamp down on corruption, and they're learning that lesson now in China. That was the smartest damn thing I've seen a big country do in a long time. You don't want to be run by a den of thieves. China is widely copying Singapore and I think it's very likely to work. They've actually shot a few people for corruption—that really gets people's attention.

Warren: Now we're starting to get some practical advice around here [laughter]. What's happened in China strikes me as totally miraculous. I never would have believed a country of that size would move so far so fast.

---

[40] Lee Kuan Yew (September 16, 1923 – March 23, 2015) was the prime minister of Singapore from 1959 to 1990, making him the longest-serving prime minister in history. During his long rule, Singapore became the most prosperous nation in Southeast Asia.

Charlie: It has never happened before in history that a country so big has come so far. Eighty percent of China was illiterate when I was a young boy. A few people made an extreme contribution to it, including the politicians in Singapore. That's all Berkshire does: copy the right people.

Warren: America's ascent to claim a massive portion of global GDP was impressive, and look at what China has done in forty years. That shows you the human potential when you find a system that unleashes it. We found it two hundred years ago and they found it forty or fifty years ago.

It's just amazing that you can have people go nowhere, basically, in their lives, for centuries, and then it explodes. It just blows me away to see it. It's the same human beings, but they found a way to unlock their potential, and I congratulate them for it. China and the U.S. will be superpowers for as far as the eye can see. I think it's imperative for two countries with nuclear weapons in this kind of world that they find a way to see the virtues and not the flaws in each other.

Q61. Station 3, San Francisco: How did you figure out the operational metrics of a new industry in which you had no previous experience?

Warren: First, we didn't have it thought out that well. But we did have a feel for it. In terms of knowing we were getting enough for our money, it was easier then.

We kept looking at things as they came along and in those days we were capital-constrained so we usually had to sell something if we wanted to buy something else. But we went with a good result when it was certain rather than trying to be hopeful about an unlikely but brilliant result.

Charlie: Part of it was because we had people that worked [together] so constructively. But there's also good timing, and we made some of our luck by being curious and seeking wisdom, and we certainly recommend that to anyone else.

It's hard to learn faster than when you get your nose whacked by a bad experience.

Warren: We had plenty of them, and the bad experiences put the good ones into perspective. But we've also had a lot of fun along the way. If you're enjoying what you're doing, you're likely to get better results than if you go to work with your teeth clenched every morning.

Charlie: It was helpful to come from a background that made it easy to identify admirable people. We have good people in the family. Both of us are indebted to them.

Warren: You still have your dad's briefcase?

Charlie: No, I don't know where it is.

Warren: I still use my dad's desk.

Q62. Station 4: How were you able to persuade your early investors that weren't family and friends to overcome doubt and fear?

Charlie: We didn't do well until we had a winning record.

Warren: I started selling stocks when I was twenty. I looked like I was sixteen and behaved like I was twelve. A lot of people who were close to me had a lot of faith in me. They knew I'd done reasonably well at that time. After I'd been investing for five or six years after leaving New York, I had enough to retire at age twenty-six. So they figured that I must have been doing something right. A lot of stuff comes along if you just keep plodding along.

Initially it was just people who knew me and had faith in me, but we started with small sums. My sister Doris and my aunt Alice invested with me. My father-in-law, William Thompson, who was a dean at the University of Nebraska at Omaha invested everything he had. Ben Graham was winding up his partnership and recommended his investors to me.

Charlie: Of course, that's the way you start [with family and friends]. The people who follow the Graham-Newman model have all done well. If you can avoid being a perfect idiot, you can do very well.

Warren: A year or two later, a doctor family friend called and introduced me to Charlie in a restaurant in Omaha. It was an accident.

Charlie: Fortunately I listened.

Q63. Station 5: Los Angeles: what matters to you most and why?

Charlie: If you're good at investing your own money, I hope you move on and do more.

I think I had an unfortunate challenge that led me into the investment world which is that I was better at figuring things out than I was at anything else and I knew I was never going to succeed as an athlete, movie star, or actor. My grandfather, Judge Munger,[41] gave me the idea that my main duty in life is to become as rational as I can be. Since I was good at that and no good at anything else, I was steered into something that worked well for me. Rationality is a moral duty. Confucius said we owe a moral duty to be rational, which is why I like Confucius. He had the same idea years ago.

Berkshire is a template of rationality. What's admired here is seeing something the way it is. To

---

[41] Thomas Charles Munger (1861–1941) was a U.S. District Court judge of Nebraska, appointed by President Theodore Roosevelt in 1907. Judge Munger and his family are described in *The Snowball: Warren Buffett and the Business of Life*, by Alice Schroeder, 2008. He is the grandfather of Charlie Munger.

me, that goes beyond building wealth; it's a moral principle.

If you have ignorance and keep it ... it's dishonorable to stay stupider than you need to be. I think you have to be generous because it is crazy not to be.

Warren: Beyond the obvious—health and family—what matters most to me is Berkshire doing well. We can't help it if the stock market declines. But I don't like to lose real money and value for the company.

Charlie: We hate losing someone else's money. How about you, Warren?

Warren: That's something that will keep me awake at night. I won't feel good. What bothers me is if I do something that actually costs Berkshire long-term value.

Charlie: A good doctor doesn't like it when a patient dies on the table.

Q64. Station 6, Sweden: What's the most intelligent question I could ask you right now?

Charlie: I don't think that's a very good question. You're asking too much of someone when you ask that.

Warren: I get asked that a lot by students.

Q65. Station 7, New York: What was the source of your investment success early on with a small amount of capital?

Warren: I had a great teacher, exceptional focus, and the right emotional discipline. I enjoyed the game.

It's actually an easy game. It does need a certain amount of IQ but it requires much more emotional stability and I went at it hammer and claw. But I was enjoying what I was doing.

From age seven to nineteen, I had the same level of enthusiasm about investment as I do now. I had a lot of enthusiasm but I didn't have any guidance or system. I hadn't been enlightened yet by the teachings of Ben Graham. Then I read *The Intelligent Investor* by Ben Graham which gave me an investment philosophy. It's fun.

Charlie: It's an easy game if you have the right temperament and you keep at it. I don't like being too much of an example to people who like being shrewd by buying and selling pieces of paper. I don't think that's a fair exchange for what you're taking out of life.

Warren: Running Berkshire is incredibly more satisfying than it was to run the partnership.

**Q66. Station 8: You had mentioned in the past that the *Wall Street Journal* had lots of competitive advantages but they were unrealized. Can you elaborate on that?

Warren: Prior to the vast spread of financial information, they had a real lock—the news ticker, for instance, was all theirs. They just totally missed what was about to happen. They never saw Michael Bloomberg coming. They didn't see areas they could have pursued that would have turned the company into something worth hundreds of billions of dollars. The company and the family money were controlled by a lawyer. The lawyers had no imagination on what to do with financial information. Everyone was getting dividends and they were happy, and they couldn't have been in a better place with a better balance sheet, but they just totally let the opportunities pass them by.

Charlie: Well, they did end up with $6–7 billion when they sold out to Rupert Murdoch. They may have blown their opportunities, but they didn't lose the family fortune.

Warren: If Tom Murphy had been dealt that hand, he could have made an enormous fortune.

Charlie: Yes, but he was more like me than he was like Bill Gates.

Warren: I don't know where he's going with that, but I would like to have the opportunity to invest in Bill retroactively.

End of Q&A session

Epilogue

As aptly stated by Bill Gates, a member of the Berkshire Hathaway board, the weekend of the AGM "is one of the most enjoyable 'duties' of my year."[42] We agree. Attending Berkshire Hathaway shareholders' meeting is one of the best ways to spend a weekend. We consider Warren Buffett's letters to the shareholders and their (Warren's and Charlie's) answers to the questions at the AGM as the best lessons in finance and investment.

You are probably reading this book because you see yourself (just as we see ourselves) as a student of value investing, specifically registered in the school of Warren Buffett and Charlie Munger. We hope if you attended the 2015 shareholders meeting, this book has been a refresher and you now have a permanent record of it so that you can revisit anytime Warren's and Charlie's perspectives on the questions that were asked. If you were not able to attend the meeting, then this is your access to the Q&A session. We hope this format will continue and we will continue to learn from these legends.

We expect the 2016 meeting to be equally informative, enlightening, fascinating, and fun. While we have no idea what questions will be asked, we expect people to be curious about decisions such as getting out of ExxonMobil, increasing the Berkshire

---

[42]   http://www.gatesnotes.com/About-Bill-Gates/Master-Class-with-Warren-Buffett-Berkshire-Hathaway-Annual-Meeting-2014

stake in IBM, Warren's and Charlie's take on President Obama's decision on Keystone XL pipeline project, the impact of falling oil prices, what plans they have for acquisitions in Europe, Charlie Munger's take on the practices of the executives of Valeant Pharmaceuticals, when to buy what and when to sell, and much more. It is definitely worth attending and we encourage all shareholders who can to attend.

As always, we expect investment wisdom that is certainly worth keeping record of. Warren and Charlie always have unusual but accurate perspectives of business and finance and it will be worth your while to hear them in their own words. We will do our best to take accurate notes and to present them in a reader-friendly form.

About the Authors

Eben Otuteye

Eben Otuteye is Professor of Finance at the University of New Brunswick, Fredericton, Canada. Professor Otuteye joined the Faculty of Business Administration at UNB in 1987 where he has been teaching various finance courses, including principles of finance, corporate finance, investments, value investing, personal financial planning, and theory of finance, in both the BBA and MBA programs.

Dr. Otuteye's research interests include behavioral finance, value investing, asset pricing models, portfolio management strategies, and the economics of e-business, topics on which he has made many conference presentations all over the world and published in several high-ranking journals.

In collaboration with Mohammad Siddiquee, Professor Otuteye developed a heuristic (the O-S heuristic) for making value investing decisions. This is a system that incorporates the value investing principles as originally propounded by Benjamin Graham and its extensions as developed and practiced by Warren Buffett and Charlie Munger.

Mohammad Siddiquee

Mohammad Siddiquee is a Lecturer in Finance at the University of New Brunswick Saint John. He studies behavioral finance as well as the psychology of decision making in investment management.

Influenced by the works of Benjamin Graham and his disciple Warren Buffett, Mohammad is also studying value investing. He is working with Dr. Otuteye on the project "Redefining Risk," which may lead to rethinking traditional risk-return paradigms.

Mohammad teaches managerial finance, investment and portfolio management, and personal financial planning in the undergraduate program, and corporate finance and entrepreneurial finance in the graduate program.

Mohammad is a PhD candidate at the University of New Brunswick. He is an avid value investor.

INDEX

www.ingramcontent.com/pod-product-compliance
Lightning Source LLC
Chambersburg PA
CBHW070811180526
45168CB00002B/581